Clarice Cliff
Price Guide

Howard and Pat Watson

Francis Joseph

ISBN 1870703 56 1

© Howard and Pat Watson and Francis Joseph Publications 1995

First impression

Published in the UK by
Francis Joseph Publications
15 St Swithuns Road, London SE13 6RW
Telephone 0181 318 9580 Facsimile 0181 318 1987

Typeset and printed, in Great Britain by
E J Folkard Print Services
199 Station Road, Crayford, Kent DA1 3QF

ISBN 1870703 56 1

Acknowledgements

The staff of Stoke-on-Trent City Library are thanked for providing access to the Clarice Cliff memorabilia in the Wilkinson Collection.
The staff of Stoke-on-Trent City Museum and Art Gallery are thanked for help with research and for essential background information.
Invaluable help in the identification and dating of patterns has been provided by Leonard R. Griffin and Louis Meisel's book *Clarice Cliff and the Bizarre Affair* and by the quarterly reviews and other publications of the Clarice Cliff Collectors Club.
Beverley and Beth Adams are warmly thanked for all their help and co-operation with photographs.
Mark Wilkinson and Jane Hay of Christie's South Kensington are also warmly thanked for supplying photographs.
Finally, all friends, dealers and customers are thanked for the interesting discussions and comments they have made to us during the preparation of this book.

Photography	**Trevor Leek and Christies South Kensington**
Cover	**Courtesy of Christies**
Production and design	**Francis Salmon**
Compilation	**Clare Ling**

How to use this book

To avoid the need for lengthy descriptions and to make reference quick and simple, every effort has been made to illustrate as many as possible of Clarice Cliff's major patterns by colour photographs.

Patterns were phased out after a long or short peiod according to popularity, and where possible the date of discontinuation has been given, but it should be noted that with tableware in particular, matchings could be ordered which would be specially decorated to the customer's requirements. In order to replace broken items, the paintress would refer to the pattern-book for designs which had become obsolete. This means that replacement items may not only be considerably later in date than the original but that also they may carry a different backstamp.

Bold words indicate a known pattern name.
Italic words indicate shapes.
If there is an unofficial popular name for a pattern this is left in normal type.

When referring to the price guide, it is important that the contents of this book be read first. The work of Clarice Cliff was not produced in a steady numbered and catalogued way, and therefore, to overcome complications, it has been necessary to put her designs into three broad ranges of popularity. From this it is possible to apply the shape of an item into one of the three ranges and come up with a price that is a broad reflection of the auction value.

When buying or selling Clarice Cliff, the collector must bear in mind that the dealer or auction house will have a mark-up on the price they are prepared to pay you. Therefore, the price you receive for a piece of Clarice Cliff, may be 20-40 per cent lower than the prices given in this book.

The main aim of any guide, though, is to give a cross-section of the market at a given time. Prices will change from day to day, but for the casual buyer, it is important to at least distinguish the pieces that are worth £5 or £50 from those that are worth £500 or £5000 and we believe that this reference guide has achieved that aim.

Contents

Introduction

For those of us who can remember a Thirties childhood, it is easy to see why Clarice Cliff's 'Bizarre Ware' came as a breath of fresh air in the days of the Depression, when the colour of Horlicks was the prevailing colour of the middle-class home. Even if we cannot remember seeing a single piece of it ourselves, we can imagine the impact it must have had. Throughout the war, the British people suffered severely from colour starvation. No wonder that in later life we turned to Clarice Cliff as eagerly as that earlier generation when she first launched her designs and took the pottery establishment by the ears.

The rediscovery of Clarice Cliff is a story in itself, and modern collectors will be forever indebted to Martin Battersby, John Jesse, Harvey Daniels, Clive Collins and a few other early enthusiasts who, along with Clarice Cliff herself, lent items for the historic 1972 exhibition at the Brighton Museum and Art Gallery which set the ball rolling. The publication by L'Odeon of *Clarice Cliff*, written by Peter Wentworth-Sheilds and Kay Johnson in 1976 was another landmark, and so was the formation by Len Griffin in 1982 of the Clarice Cliff Collectors Club.

My own collection was begun in 1982 when on holiday in Harrogate I bought a small *Tulips* vase for £4. Attracted by her brilliant use of shape and colour, I collected more pieces and gathered more background knowledge, coming to realise the extent of Clarice Cliff's influence on pottery design and the skill with which she drew on an enormously wide range of sources for her inspiration, from the flowers and scenery around her Potteries home to the classic Art Deco styles of the day.

Some pieces turned up in unusual places – a **Gibraltar** *Bonjour* jug holding back curtains on a windowsill, a **Tulip** *and* **Leaves** plaque almost thrown away because it no longer fitted in with a new colour scheme, a **Red Roofs** vase offered over the phone by the original owner. Not long afterwards, Channel 4's 'Pottery Ladies' series aroused considerable public interest, and Clarice Cliff's name was beginning to be a household word again, as it had been in the Thirties.

Soon it became clear that an illustrated guide to her work would be welcome, as a handy pocket reference book for collectors to use to identify patterns and shapes, and to provide a pictorial introduction to the work of Clarice Cliff in general, and in 1988 *Collecting Clarice Cliff* was published, followed by *The Colourful World of Clarice Cliff*. With both these books now out of print, the present book offers the information they contained, updated and with an entirely new set of photographs plus an up-to-date, enlarged price guide, together with a selection of backstamps to aid dating.

The aim once again has been to be concise and practical, but at the same time to illustrate the astonishing range and variety of the work of the woman who will always be, for me and for thousands of other collectors, the greatest of all our Pottery Ladies – Clarice Cliff.

Howard Watson.

Clarice Cliff – The Sunshine Girl

They called her 'the Sunshine Girl', and the colourful hand-painted pottery she designed was hailed as 'Happy China'. Today Clarice Cliff needs no introduction to collectors of Art Deco ceramics, and media attention has made her name once more a household word. One of the outstanding women designers of her era, she was internationally famous during her own lifetime and lived to see her pottery beginning to be eagerly collected in the early Seventies. Her prolific range of patterns and shapes and her fairy-tale life story have made her into a Potteries legend, and her facsimile signature now guarantees a good price – sometimes a sensationally high price – when it turns up at a London auction or on the Antiques Roadshow.

Though she was born in the final year of the last century there was nothing remotely Victorian about Clarice Cliff. Her ideas were well in advance of her own day, and though often imitated since have never been surpassed. She grew up, along with two brothers and five sisters, in a typical Potteries working-class family in Tunstall, Stoke-on-Trent. In later years she remembered as the high-spot of her schooldays the weekly half-hour drawing lessons and being "entrusted to make large papier mâché maps built up on nails of varying heights, and coloured, for use in geography lessons". At thirteen, like most children in the area, she left school to go to work, taking up an apprenticeship at Lingard, Webster and Company, to be taught free-hand painting on pottery. From there, she went to another factory, Hollingshead and Kirkham, to learn lithography, a form of transfer decoration, finally moving in 1916 to Wilkinson's Royal Staffordshire Pottery, where she was to remain for the rest of her career. In the evenings she went to classes at the Tunstall School of Art and on Sundays she taught at the local Sunday School. A vivacious brunette, she had a flair for stylish dressing, making many of her own clothes herself, and for interior decoration. Orange, yellow, gold and black were the colours she chose for her bedroom, which must have made it unique in the backstreets of Tunstall.

At Wilkinsons the apprentices were given training in modelling, gilding, firing and pottery design, along with the keeping of shape and pattern books. The decorating manager, Jack Walker, kept an eye on their developing skills and guided them into the department best suited to their talents. After seeing a free-hand picture of a butterfly painted in a spare moment by Clarice Cliff, and following a consultation with Colley Shorter, the firm's managing director, he put her to work alongside two of his chief designers, Fred Ridgeway and John Butler. Her task was "very fine filigree gilding with a pen, tracing spiders' webs, butterflies etc. to hide small imperfections on expensive ware". Now in her mid-twenties, this gave her a certain amount of status, as well as increased wages, which meant she could affort to take the step, unusual for those days, of moving into a flat of her own. In no time she had transformed it to suit her advanced ideas – a pink and blue bedroom, a bathroom in yellow and black.

Even more important was the decision on the part of the management to send her for a short course in sculpture at the Royal College of Art in London. There she worked hard, creating a good impression on the authorities. Her course tutor, Professor Ledward, reported that "she has natural ability as a modeller ... and would derive very great benefit from a longer period of continuous study". The Registrar also considered that there was "no doubt that she has native ability" and wrote to assure Colley Shorter that "we should be pleased to admit her again". Eager to put her new ideas into practice, Clarice returned to the Potteries, where she now had a studio awaiting her at Newport Pottery, adjoining Wilkinson's main factory. Since its takeover by Wilkinsons in 1920, shelves piled high with dated stocks of whiteware had gathered dust in Newport Pottery, but now its time had come. "This huge stock," Clarice Cliff wrote years later, "had always interested me, and presented a challenge!". In rising to that challenge she transformed not only her own career but the fortunes of her employers, then at a low ebb, and in so doing earned for herself a place in the history of British pottery.

The Birth of Bizarre

Faced by the dusty whiteware, Clarice visualised it transformed by the application of bright colours in bold geometric designs. Beginning with diamonds, triangles and banding in a variety of combinations, the patterns she devised were within the limited capabilities of the young apprentices who could be spared to take part in the experiment. Considerable care was taken to preserve secrecy, and not until over seven hundred pieces had been decorated was the range launched, in the Autumn of 1928, under the name of *Bizarre Ware*, chosen by Clarice herself. Her own name was added to the backstamp, an accolade which put her on equal terms with the select band of acknowledged ceramic artists like Charlotte Rhead, Susie Cooper and Mollie Hancock. Not everyone at the factory was so confident, however – the firm's salesmen, used to taking traditional patterns round to their customers, regarded the new range with doubt and derision. To their astonishment they found that on a trial run it was welcomed as an attractive novelty, and sold quickly. More paintresses were added to the Bizarre team and the patterns and colours were standardised to speed up production. Variations on the regular geometric designs led to the use of sweeping curves and blocks of strong colour in abstract shapes to satisfy the demand for "colour and plenty of it ... I cannot put too much of it into my designs to please women", as Clarice herself said at the time. Continual change, too, she knew, was the order of the day. All the pottery manufacturers in the area – and there were four hundred factories competing for orders – constantly brought out new ranges to catch the customer's eye, ranges they advertised in the trade journal, the *Pottery Gazette and Glass Trades Review* and which they put on display at the annual London trade fairs and in the leading department stores. Before long, Clarice and her Bizarre Girls were travelling the country to give in-store demonstrations of their methods, so that the public and the press could admire the skill which went into the production of this exciting new range.

For Clarice Cliff, of course, the success of Bizarre Ware meant much more than commercial viability, important though that was. It is difficult today, with very different social attitudes, to imagine how much was at stake personally for her. Its creation had involved her in many weeks of close co-operation with Colley Shorter, a much older married man with an invalid wife, and inevitably their growing intimacy had become the subject of speculation and gossip on the part of workers and the management team alike. Had Colley Shorter formed an association with a woman considered to be his social equal and well away from the factory setting, probably little notice would have been taken of the situation. As it was, Clarice had laid herself open to barely-concealed disapproval on all sides, and if she failed the future looked bleak. There would be many jealous observers only too glad to see her taken down a peg or two. Only success, overwhelming success, could ensure her survival, and fortunately her gamble paid off. Her relief must have been enormous – she had succeeded beyond her wildest dreams. At last a secure future lay ahead, ending eventually, after his wife's death, in marriage to the man who had trusted in her talent and launched her on her brilliant career. No wonder she worked long and hard to ensure that her success continued: she was spurred on by the knowledge that things might easily have been very different indeed.

Crocus and After

Floral patterns followed the early geometric and abstract designs, starting with the *Crocus* range, which was so popular that *Lupin,* next to it in the pattern book, was never put into full production and is now extremely rare. In its various colourways, on both conventional existing shapes, and on the striking modern shapes Clarice designed herself, *Crocus* had a lively immediate appeal which made it a continuous best-seller throughout the Thirties. More floral patterns – *Gayday, Lily, Gardenia* and *Cowslip* – were added, and as the skills of her paintresses increased Clarice introduced stylised landscapes, many of them featuring quaint cottages nestled among colourful trees and bushes. By now all the main stores and china shops across the country stocked her ware, and such was the demand that a new name, *Fantasque,* was coined for part of Newport's output.

"*Bizarre* was usually sold to one customer in a town, so *Fantasque* was supposed to be a little different and sold to another shop", she wrote. Experiments in decorative techniques and surface textures led to new variations such as *Latona* and *Inspiration* (1929), *Scraphito, Applique* and *Delecia* (1930), *Cafe au Lait, Nuage* and *Damask Rose* (1931) and *Patina* (1932). As fashions changed, the hard-edged hand-painting technique was supplemented by the softer 'etching' a blending of brush-strokes used for patterns like *Rhodanthe, Viscaria, Aurea* and *Tralee* (1934-5) and the moulded ranges, *My Garden* and *Celtic Harvest*, came into their own.

Besides the tableware, vases and plaques that were the bread-and-butter lines of the factory, facemasks, figurines and novelty items appeared in a continual stream, evidence that Clarice Cliff had never lost her interest in and enjoyment of modelling in clay. From time to time, too, this was combined with experiments with glazes, so that some pieces were issued in a commercial combination of colours, like cream and gilt, but also in a restrained celadon grey-green. The *Goldstone* range, too, though usually found with rather crude decoration, can sometimes be seen with simple lining which looks stunningly modern and sophisticated.

Although Wilkinsons and Newport Pottery were both in the happy position of full order-books, the state of the industry overall was giving cause for concern. In 1932 an experiment was initiated which was designed to involve leading artists of the day in creating patterns for use on pottery and china. The collaboration between Laura Knight and Clarice Cliff was particularly fruitful and these are the pieces which today fetch very high prices. At the time, however, the experiment was not a success, partly because, however famous, the artists lacked confidence in designing for an unknown medium and so tended to be timid, and partly because the public did not respond with much enthusiasm, perhaps feeling that they were having highbrow art foisted upon them in disguise. Only a very few of the items in this range can match up to the originality and exuberance of Clarice Cliff's own designs, and no doubt she found it frustrating to have to spend so much time on an exercise she may well have realised from the start was doomed to failure.

The Later Years

Though her earliest ranges were gradually phased out, *Fantasque* in 1934 and *Bizarre* in 1937, Clarice's own success continued right up until the outbreak of war at the end of 1939. Colley Shorter's marketing expertise meant that she was constantly in the public eye and that her many celebrity customers from the world of stage, screen and radio were shown in the press at the factory or at London trade shows collecting goods they had ordered. The firm's scrap-book, now in the Wilkinson Archives at Stoke-on-Trent City Library, Hanley, is full of photographs and press cuttings of these occasions, which must have made a welcome break in the daily routine. Popular women's magazines like 'Woman's Journal' commissioned exclusive sets of dinner and tea-ware for their readers, and carried embroidery transfers and crochet patterns for table-mats or afternoon tea-cloths to complement Clarice Cliff pottery.

For their time, it seems likely that Wilkinsons were on the whole good employers. Though like most factories of the day the workshops were dark and dismal, the Bizarre girls were allowed a radio and sang while they worked, a concession which sent production up by twenty-five per cent. Works outings were arranged to local beauty spots, and the firm took part in the 'Crazy Day' carnival parades in aid of charity. Trips to give demonstrations in London and elsewhere varied the routine for some of the girls, and thanks to the constant demand for their skills they all had job security, which meant a lot in those days. The paintresses had a certain status as members of the Bizarre team, and if they later remembered Clarice as a stickler for time-keeping and strict in her insistence on quality control, this made good business sense and ultimately was for their benefit. Anyone who remembers the factory floor of the

Thirties knows that long hours, low wages and grim working conditions were the norm, not only in the Potteries.

Certainly there is no denying that Clarice worked as hard as anyone. With over two thousand patterns to her credit, as well as around five hundred new shapes, she had a formidable volume of work behind her when war came and the main factory was turned over to the production of undecorated hotel-ware, Newport becoming a government store. Her vivid colours and unexpected shapes had brightened the whole decade, had kept her employers on an even keep and ensured that the shadow of the dole queue never threatened her fellow-workers.

Drawing her inspiration, like all designers, from everything that came her way (the Staffordshire countryside, gardening books and art magazines to name but a few), she had kept up a constant creative output week in, week out. Now came the opportunity to settle down at last. With the death of Colley Shorter's wife, marriage soon followed and she became the mistress of a superb Art Nouveau house set in beautiful grounds. Though she continued to work on the administrative side of the factory for a time after the war, she sold the business to Midwinters shortly after being widowed in 1963 and devoted herself to her home and garden. In 1972, the year of her death, an exhibition of her work at Brighton Museum marked the beginning of the Clarice Cliff revival, and she provided notes for the catalogue and several pieces for display. More than forty years had passed since she launched her Happy China on an unsuspecting world. No doubt she smiled to think that what had then been a commercial gamble and a personal triumph was now part of pottery history, and that Clarice Cliff, the Sunshine Girl, had become the doyenne of Art Deco.

Pat Watson

Collecting Clarice Cliff

One of the most intriguing aspects of collecting Clarice Cliff is the knowledge that it was originally regarded as cheap, cheerful pottery for practical use in the home. Bought in vast quantities in the Thirties, few realised how popular the quirky colours and bold designs would become — not only as 'happy' household items, but artistic treasures admired by thousands of collectors worldwide.

At the same time, it was at variance with the conventional tableware of the day, and putting it on the market at all was a gamble. Sheer chance, backed up by a clever advertising strategy, meant that what began as an experiment quickly turned into a phenomenon. The name *Bizarre* says it all.

With the benefit of hindsight, it is easy to trace all kinds of influences which may have played a part in providing inspiration for particular shapes and patterns. Like all commercial designers, Clarice Cliff studied current trends and fashions, altering them to suit her purpose and taking into account the limitations of her material and the skills of her workforce. Her designs increased in complexity as production gathered momentum — from geometric to abstract, from abstract to floral, from floral to landscape — always with colour lavishly used to brighten up the drab interiors of her day.

The sensational success of Bizarre Ware, particularly in a period of economic hardship, is proof enough that Clarice Cliff shrewdly assessed the climate of the times and was fulfilling a need for colourful and original pottery which stood out from the tableware on offer from other manufacturers in the industry. Not afraid to take risks, she offered bored housewives something new, and in so doing created patterns and shapes which were to hold their appeal for all time.

For collectors today, particularly the design conscious, her work has many attractions. Unlike buyers in the Thirties, we now have the whole range at once to choose from, an endless variety of individual items, all instantly recognisable and each with its own special characteristics. Limited only by considerations of space and price-range, we can select the pieces we prefer from more than two thousand patterns and five hundred shapes, and seldom these days does the functional purpose enter into a purchase. When did you last put lupins in your **Lotus** jug, or teabags into your **Stamford** teapot?

An added pleasure is the search. Not for us the routine shopping trip into the Thirties High Street to a china shop with shelves crammed with brand new Clarice Cliff pottery. Instead we have the excitement of the early morning arrival at the antique fair, the long hours spent at the auction house, the leisurely browsing while on holiday, any of which may yield an unforeseen treasure, or equally, prove fruitless. No jumble-sale can be passed by, no junk shop, however unpromising, can be left unexplored, for, as every collector is aware, you never know . . .

We all have our own great 'finds', that elusive piece with only the faintest hairline tucked away on the top shelf of the local charity shop, or the incredible discovery at the school fête, with only a few slight chips. Collectors are the eternal optimists, like avid gardeners who believe in the pictures on the front of the seed packets. And who can blame them? For after all, whatever the weather may be elsewhere, in the world of Clarice Cliff, the sun is always shining.

Surface Techniques

Hand-painted pottery, especially on-glaze hand-painting, has a spontaneity impossible to obtain by mechanical means.

Part of the charm of Clarice Cliff pottery lies in the minute variations which resulted from the pattern being copied by different paintresses at different times. The original design was copied from the pattern book, but as speed was the inevitable priority due to piecework rates, the paintresses sometimes worked from memory. This lead to slight changes in outline, but did not affect colours as they were standardised.

The hand-painting was carried out on ware previously glazed with 'Honeyglaze', a warm cream glaze specially mixed for Bizarre Ware. After decoration, the ware was fired for 12 hours to harden the enamel paint used.

Patterns like *Crocus* were painted in colour, free-hand, but more elaborate patterns were first outlined in Indian ink, which evaporated during firing. Varieties of *Crocus* included *Original Crocus* (sometimes called *Autumn Crocus*), in purple, blue and orange, *Spring Crocus* in pastel shades, *Sungleam* in orange and yellow, *Blue Crocus* and *Purple Crocus* in single colours and *Peter Pan Crocus*, which was the original design with a black silhouette of a tree added. Later variations included placing the croci in a bunch at the side of the ware, and even coming downwards from the rims of cups and jugs.

Other glazes besides 'Honeyglaze' were used to create special effects for new ranges. *Latona* was a milky glaze with an egg-shell finish which, combined with a number of specifically designed floral and geometric patterns that featured large areas of solid colour, achieved a subtle brilliance, quite unlike the *Bizarre* range with its more direct impact.

The *Inspiration* range was created with a mixture of metallic oxide glazes to produce striking results in deep blues, turquoises, pinks and pale mauves. As the thin glaze tended to run, the pottery often became glued to the kiln funiture, causing time-consuming problems for the trimmers. Consequently, it was expensive and made in limited quantities.

Similarly, the *Applique* range was costly, as the designs, painted in sumptuous colours (probably especially bought in), covered almost the entire surface of the ware. Vivid landscapes predominated, each with a castle, a windmill, a bridge or a stylised tree as the focal point, and it is this range which now fetches the highest prices at auction, being both rare and outstandingly attractive.

Much more widely used was the Cafe Au Lait technique, which being applied with a sponge gave a stippled surface to the pottery before a pattern was added on top or on an area left free from the stippling. Though its name suggests that only brown paint was used, yellow, green, orange and blue were also used very effectively.

Another successful technique was *Delecia*, which was originally comprised of random drippings of thin paint in a mixture of colours and was later combined with bands of fruit or flowers. Several factories used this method of covering the surface, but the stylish designs which came later are unique to Clarice Cliff. A popular landscape, *Forest Glen*, has *Delecia* as its background, while *Cherry Blossom* has a tree with white flowers against similar red and green runnings.

In *Nuage*, thickened paint was used to give a texture like orange peel, combined with bold, simple motifs that were produced with stencils, while *Damask Rose* aimed at the opposite effect, a perfectly smooth pink glaze with small decorations, which being difficult to apply, was produced only briefly. *Patina* went further than *Nuage*, as liquid clay or 'slip' was mixed with the paint to give a rough surface, on top of which the patterns, ususally simple landscapes, were applied after glazing. Also uneven in surface, but no doubt much easier to decorate, was the *Scraphito* range, on which abstract designs were moulded deeply into the ware and then picked out in bold colours.

In the mid-Thirties, for the pattern *Rhodanthe* and its colour variations *Aurea* and *Viscaria*, and also for the thatched roof of *Trallee*, a method of blending brushstrokes of colour to create a shaded effect was used. Known as 'etching', this resulted in a softer, more subtle effect which was in keeping with popular taste. About this time the *Raffia* range was also launched. In this method the surface of the pottery was moulded to appear like woven raffia, a familiar handicraft material of the day, and colour was applied in patches in various combinations against glazes in pastel green and beige.

For *Goldstone*, a different type of body clay was used and a speckled surface achieved by mixing metallic dust into the glaze. Sometimes the decoration was restrained and the ware has the appearance of modern studio pottery, while other items have a rather garish form of decoration giving a dated look.

But perhaps the two ranges which most clearly indicate that the vivid colours of Clarice Cliff's early work had, for the time being, lost their appeal for contemporary purchasers are *My Garden* and *Celtic Harvest*. In January 1934, two years before the range began, Wilkinsons' took an advertisement in a publication for gardeners called *My Garden*, in which they described the *Goldstone* vases illustrated as being "designed by a lover of flowers for flower lovers". so quite possibly that was the origin of the name.

Popular both now and in their own day, *My Garden* with its pretty, unsophisticated colours and moulded flowers, and *Celtic Harvest* with its encrusted fruit on handles and lids, were in production throughout the late Thirties and in the post-war years. Though they do not hold for collectors the strong appeal of early *Bizarre* shapes and patterns, they nevertheless illustrate the skill with which Clarice Cliff, as always, tailored her designs to satisfy prevailing taste, true to the adage of the day that 'the customer is always right' and reminding us that she was involved, first and foremost, in a commercial undertaking, in which she needed all her proven creative versatility to survive in a tough competitive marketplace.

Backstamps

So many and so varied are the backstamps to be found on Clarice Cliff pottery that they may well appear at first to be more of a hindrance than a help in deciding the date of any particular piece.

However, as long as collectors are not too dogmatic, backstamps can be a useful guide and a few general rules can be established.

Do not, for instance, be misled by impressed dates, since these refer to the date of manufacture of the pottery, not the date of its decoration. These two dates could be months or even a year or more apart. The hand-painted, stamped or lithographed information is what is relevant to the decoration.

Totally hand-painted marks can be found only on very early ware (i.e, the Original Bizarre) and only the earliest of these items do not credit Clarice Cliff. It was not long before her name was added, probably as an additional sales gimmick, to all wares. Colley Shorter must have been relieved that this talented protégé had a name which was easy to remember and with a good commercial ring. 'Handpainted Bizarre by Clarice Cliff, Newport Pottery, England' both sounded and read well in advertising and other promotional literature.

Once success was assured, a rubber stamp was used to speed up the marking process. At first this was quite a large size but later it was smaller and neater. These can be distinguished from later (1931) lithographs by the fuzzy outline of the rubber stamp and also, in some cases, by the colour of the ink used, since gilt and pale green occasionally appear as well as the usual black.

Even when lithographs, (which are pre-printed transfers), came into common use, pattern and range names were often added by hand, at first in script and later in block letters – unless the popularity of the pattern justified a lithograph of its own. Early *Crocus* and *Gayday* items have handwritten pattern names, while later pieces carry a lithograph of the name. Similarly, items with 'Registration applied for' obviously pre-date those with the eventual registration number added.

Bizarre Ware became increasingly popular, and from 1930 onwards some pottery was issued crediting Wikinson's rather than the Newport Pottery. This was in order to spread tax liability. *Fantasque* as a range name was used between 1929 and 1934, at first on its own in two sizes, and later in combination with Bizarre, initially rubberstamped and later, from 1931 onwards, lithographed.

Biarritz, introduced in 1933, also had its own lithograph mark, and was used with a Newport or Wilkinson's backstamp according to where the piece was decorated, the Newport pieces having a Clarice Cliff or Bizarre mark added.

In the mid-Thirties, Clarice Cliff became involved in a time-consuming and far from successful experiment intended to involve leading artists of the day in the production of designs for tableware. Since a facsimile of the artist's signature was often included along with other backstamps, these are an interesting reminder of a well-meaning but misguided attempt to bring fine art to the dining table.

Among the artists involved were Dame Laura Knight, painter of fairground and circus subjects, Duncan Grant and Vanessa Bell of the Bloomsbury Group of artists and writers, Paul Nash who exhibited with the Surrealists, and Eva Crofts, the textile designer, as well as many others equally diverse. Gordon M Forsyth, from 1920 to 1945 Superintendent of Art Instruction in Stoke on Trent and an important influence on many pottery designers, also contributed to the experiment, the results of which eventually went on display in London in 1934 as 'Modern Art for the Table'. It later toured the country and it was taken to Australia.

Other interesting backstamps collectors may come across are those put on ware produced especially for stores like Harrods, Lawleys and Brice Rogers, whose orders were so large it was worthwhile adding their name on each item or, as in the case of Brice Rogers, a tiny picture of a quaint thatched cottage with the words, "Brice Rogers Cottage Pottery". The women's magazine, 'Woman's Journal', also commissioned patterns exclusive to their readers, and these dinner and tea sets occasionally appear in auction, identified by a backstamp giving the name of the magazine.

Finally however, after both the Bizarre and Fantasque marks had been phased out, various Clarice Cliff marks appeared alone, sometimes as lithographs and sometimes embossed on the ware itself. From 1941 the Newport mark was no longer used, as the factory had been requisitioned for the duration by the government, and once the sale of the factories to Midwinters was completed in 1964, all backstamps ceased. The plethora of backstamps tell a complicated story, and often add to the confusion, for it is possible to find a 23 piece tea-set of which only one item, perhaps the milk jug, carries any marks at all, while on another tiny item, like a coffee-cup, a wealth of backstamps may cover every scrap of space.

Nevertheless, together with a knowledge of pattern and shape chronology, backstamps can shed at least some light on the years when Clarice Cliff was at her busiest, little dreaming that 50 years later her work would be sought after by collectors worldwide.

Howard Watson

Currently one of Clarice Cliff's most popular landscapes, **May Avenue** reflects the influence of the Cubist painters in its spade-shaped black trees. (Beverley)

Another vivid stylised landsape — **Sunray.** (Beverley)

The slender black tree-trunks of **Blue Firs** emphasise the shape of this tall vase. (Beverley)

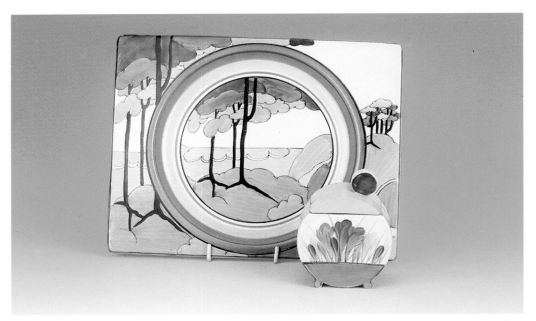

A Biarritz plate showing imaginative use of the **Blue Firs** pattern, with the rare **Blue Crocus** pattern on a Bonjour shape jampot. (Beverley)

Coral Firs, the alternative colourway, worked equally well on all shapes, here on a double candle holder, a conical bowl and a *Bonjour* shape jampot. (Beverley)

More landscape variations — **Pink Roof Cottage** on the left, **Gibraltar** on a decorative plate centre, and another pastel landscape on the right. (Beverley)

A **Propeller** jardinière and a **Sliced Circle** *Isis* vase. (Beverley)

Two colourful plates — **Autumn** on the left and **Melon**, once called by collectors "Picasso Fruit", on the right. (Beverley)

Two landscapes, **Luxor** and **Summerhouse**. (Beverley)

The *Appliqué* range is now very collectable. **Red Tree** on the left is a good example, shown here with a **Sunray** plate. (Beverley)

Contrasting landscapes — **Tulips** on the left, **Etna** on the right. (Beverley)

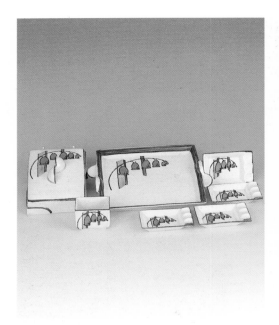

A smoker's set, decorated with **Solomon's Seal**. (Beverley)

A **Lido Lady** ashtray and a comical spotted cat. (Beverley)

The *Age of Jazz* figures, designed as a table decoration for use when listening to the wireless . . . (Beverley)

. . . and two toby jugs, the traditional Toby Fillpot and Don Quixote. (Beverley)

Don Quixote appears again here with a selection of other novelties — the Teepee teapot, designed by M. B. Sylvester, a Winston Churchill toby jug, a Golliwog toothbrush holder and a pair of pixie bookends. (Christies)

More bookends here — the **Student and the Showgirl** flank a wallmask of a girl in a green beret, while the *L'Oiseau* bookends have a *Teddy Bear* bookend between them, his base decorated with the *Sunburst* pattern. (Right) Star signs were a popular wall decoration. (Christies)

Subway Sadie here is a hat-pin holder. The *Duck* egg-cup set is decorated with a **Geometric** pattern. (Beverley)

More bookends, this time in **Sunrise**, with a **Luxor** vase. (Christies)

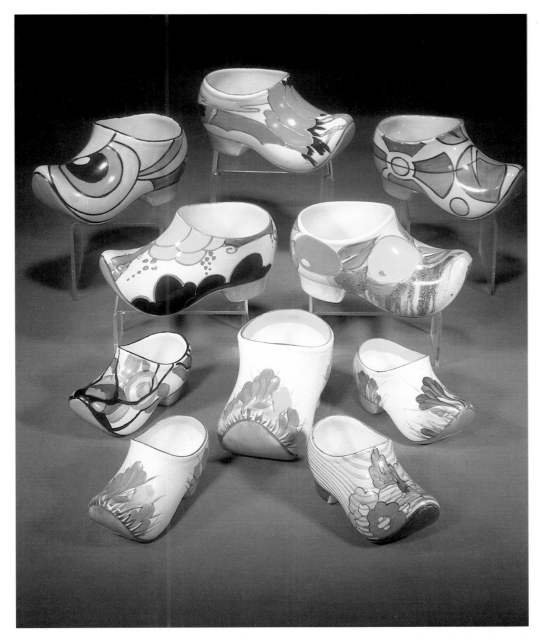

Sabots, or clogs, make a striking collection — top row in **Propeller**, **Solitude** and **Swirls**, with **Delecia Citrus** and **Summerhouse** below. **Blue Crocus** is next to **Sungleam Crocus** with **Circle Tree** on the right, and **Capri** in the foreground is next to the smaller size in **Sungleam Crocus**. (Christies)

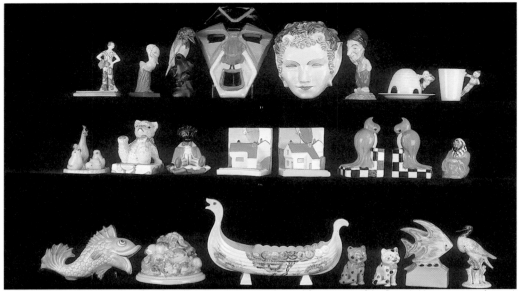

Novelties galore — the *Lido Lady* in **Blue Chintz** lounging pyjamas, a *Mother Duck* figurine, a *Kingfisher* flower-holder, a grotesque facemask (designed by Ron Birks), a facemask modelled as an exotic woman's head, a figurine of an old Dutchman, a *Goblin* nightlight and a *Pixie* mug in the top row, in the centre row a *Cockerel and Chick* cruet, *Teddy Bear* and *Golliwog* bookends, *Cottage* bookends, green *L'Oiseau* bookends and an *Arab* figurine, and in the bottom row a wallpocket in the shape of a comical fish, a table-centre modelled as a pile of fruit, a *Viking Longboat* in **Viscaria**, two laughing cats, an *Angelfish* flower-holder and a wading bird flower-holder. (Christies)

A collection of jampots — Row 1: **Rudyard**, **Circle Tree**, **Tulip and Leaves**, **Melon**, **Idyll**, **Autumn Crocus**, stylised leaves with a crescent moon motif, **Gardenia**, **Secrets**, and **Forest Glen**. Row 2: **Oranges**, **Gibraltar**, **Nasturtium**, **Secrets**, **Solitude**, **Delecia Pansy**, a naive drawing of a ship by Joan Shorter, **Double V** and **Forest Glen**. Row 3: **Pink Tree**, an unusual version of **Blue Chintz**, **Peter Pan Crocus**, **Oranges**, **Autumn Crocus**, **Floral Nuage**, **Rhondanthe**, and **Trees and House**. (Christies)

28

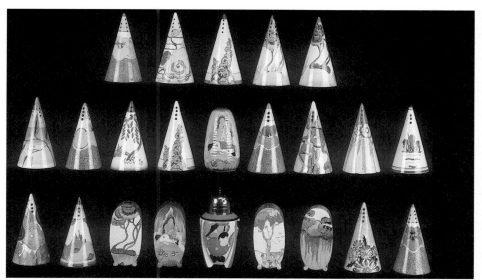

Sugar sifters, especially in the *Conical* shape, are very popular. Here we have Row 1: **Nasturtium**, **Amberose**, **Sunshine**, **Aurea** and **Rhodanthe**. Row 2: **Kelverne**, **Nasturtium**, a tree in shades of brown and red, **Sunshine**, **Forest Glen**, **Nasturtium**, **Blue Chintz**, **Delecia Daisy** and **Autumn Crocus**, and Row 3: **Blue Chintz**, **Secrets**, **Rhodanthe**, **Forest Glen**, **Orange Chintz**, **Delecia Pansy**, **Marguerite** and **Nasturtium**. (Christies)

A mixture of teapot shapes, row 1: **Delecia Citrus**, **Autumn Crocus**, **Damask Rose** with a motif of oranges, a **Geometric** pattern in orange, yellow and black, and simple banding on the *Lynton* shape. Row 2: **Aurea**, **Secrets**, **Autumn Crocus**, **Rhodanthe**, **Idyll**, **Coral Firs**, **Autumn Crocus** again and **Oranges**. (Christies)

The *Stamford* teapot shape again, this time as part of a Tea for Two in **Red Roofs**.
(Christies)

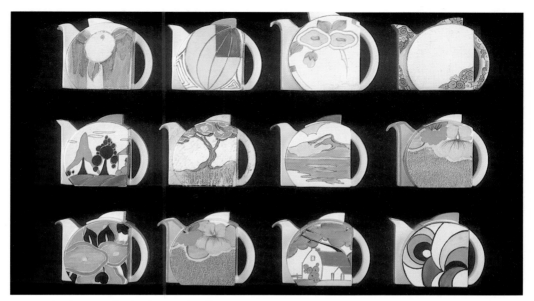

It was a shape which showed off every pattern well. Row 1: **Delecia Citrus**, **Melon**, stylised yellow flowers, tiny stylised flowers. Row 2: **Trees and House**, **Patina Tree**, **Gibraltar**, **Nasturtium** and Row 3: **Orange Chintz**, **Nasturtium**, **Red Roofs** and **Swirls**.

The *Bonjour* shape is striking here in **Oranges and Lemons**, with a solid-handled cup and saucer and two sizes of plate. (Beverley)

Jugs came in a similar variety of shapes, Row 1: **Blue Chintz**, **Autumn**, **Kelverne**, **Honolulu** and **Lydiat**, Row 2: a novelty jug with a circus performer jumping through a hoop, **Pastel Autumn**, a *Dragon Jug* in green and orange and one in **Original Delecia**. (Christies)

Row 1: *Summerhouse, Orange Roof Cottage, Garland* (one of a set of three); Row 2: *Trees and House, Rhodanthe*, the other two sizes of *Garland*, and *Blue W*; Row 3: *Autumn Crocus, Trees and House, Forest Glen, Autumn* and *Bridgewater Orange*.

Honolulu, once known as Tiger Tree, worked equally well on traditional shapes like the *Athens* jug and on new shapes like *Stamford*. (Christies)

Pastel Autumn was also very versatile. (Christies)

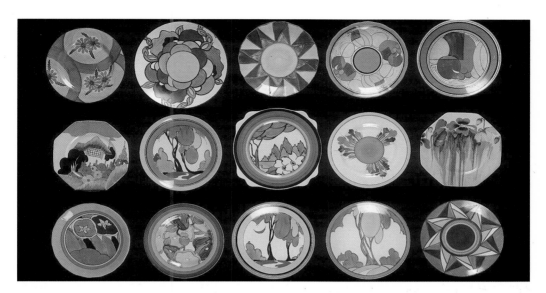

But perhaps plates offered the paintresses the best surface, Row 1: two varieties of **Melon**, an early geometric pattern, **Latona** with a design of semi-circular sections and stylised leaves, **Blue Ribbon**; Row 2: **Delecia Poppy**, **Autumn Crocus**, **Limberlost**, **Autumn** and **Trallee**; Row 3: an early geometric pattern, **Pastel Autumn**, **Autumn**, **Blue Chintz** and **Gardenia**. (Christies)

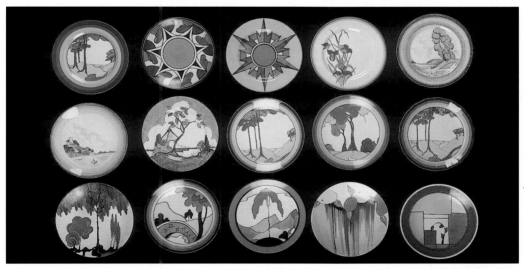

Row 1: **Coral Firs**, **Double V**, an early geometric pattern, a spray of **Slipper Orchids**, a lakeside *Crayon* landscape. Row 2: a *Crayon* habour scene, **Blue Japan**, **Coral Firs**, **Orange Autumn**, **Coral Firs**, and Row 3: **Latona Tree**, **House and Bridge**, **Etna**, **Delecia Citrus** and **Branch and Squares**. (Christies)

Coffee sets make a superb display — here, **Red Gardenia** with matching vases and a large plaque. (Christies)

A *Conical* shape coffee set in the very rare **Appliqué Avignon**. (Christies)

A part coffee-set with a matching cauldron in the bold Geometric pattern now known as **Sunburst**. (Christies)

More from the *Appliqué* range — an Appliqué Avignon vase with two Appliqué Windmill items and a **Sunray** plate. (Beverley)

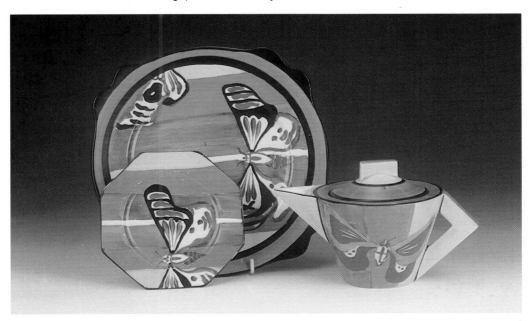

Striking examples of the **Butterfly** pattern. (Beverley)

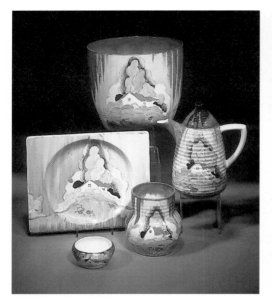

Left: Combining **Delecia**-type drips with a cottage landscape, **Forest Glen** is seen here with an example of the alternate colourway, **Newlyn**, which has a blue sky. Right: A large wall-plate in **Forest Glen**. (Beverley)

A plate, vase and *Bonjour* jampot, also in **Forest Glen**. (Beverley)

Appliqué Lucerne is shown here in two colourways, the large plate with an orange sky and blue roofs, the *Conical* cup with a blue sky and red roofs, while the **Appliqué Lugano** octagonal plate has an orange sky. The *Athens* jug is in **Appliqué Red Tree**. (Christies)

Trees and House, seen here on a *Conical* jug, makes an unusual geometric pattern when used as the interior decoration on the accompanying bowl. In the foreground is a **Forest Glen** biscuit barrel and a **Luxor** jug. (Beverley)

Two attractive landscapes, **Alton** and **Autumn**. (Beverley)

Summerhouse, another popular landscape, this time on a jardinière. (Beverley)

A single-handled *Lotus* jug in **Devon**, with two small vases, **Berries** on the left and **Sunrise** on the right, with a small jardinière in **Appliqué Palermo** behind it. (Beverley)

Banding was often used to good effect along with a landscape pattern like **Honolulu**. (Beverley)

The effect worked very well on *Biarritz* plates — **Idyll** on the left and **Windbells** on the right. (Beverley)

Idyll is seen again on this *Bonjour Tea for Two*, with interesting variations in the pose and dress of the crinoline lady, a popular motif of the 1930s. (Christies)

She is featured again on this assortment of **Idyll** items. (Christies)

Another romantic **Appliqué** subject was the gypsy caravan. It rests beneath a twisted tree bearing large oranges, and is known as **Appliqué Caravan**. Also shown is the colourful **Circle Tree** and in the foreground a planter decorated with geometric shapes. (Beverley)

A selection of Conical shakers, backed by three interesting vase shapes. (Beverley)

More interesting plates, top left **Red Flower**; top right, **Trees and House**, bottom row from left: **Wax Flower, Applique Avignon, Delecia Citrus** and **Orange Autumn**. (Beverley)

A large Cubes plate with an **Orange House** *Stamford* teapot. (Beverley)

Another single-handed *Lotus* jug in **Red Roofs**, with a vase painted in a geometric pattern of blue, yellow and orange triangles. (Beverley)

A **Melon** plate and a **Blue W** conical jug. (Beverley)

Two triangular items — a **Melon** vase and a **Poplar** planter. (Beverley)

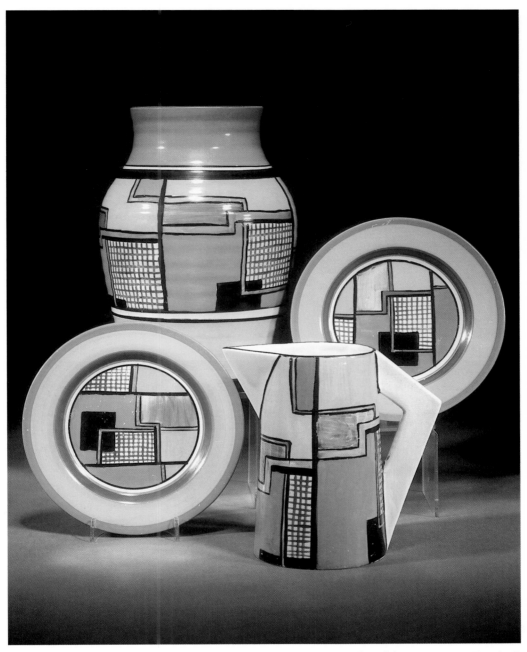

Sporting motifs were not neglected — here, some colourful pieces in *Football*.
(Christies)

Tennis was also a popular pastime in the 1930s and this abstract pattern is known as **Tennis**. (Christies)

Two single-handled Lotus jugs in **Tennis** frame an **Appliqué Lucerne** jardinière and **Autumn** vase, with in the foreground a *Secrets* plate and a **Blue W** plate with a **Boy Blue** milk jug and a **Devon** *Conical* sugar sifter between them. (Christies)

Blue W again, this time on a single-handled *Lotus* jug. (Christies)

Stunning examples of the Cubist landscape **Sunray**, showing banding variations .

Lotus jugs and Isis vases: Row 1: **Kelverne**, **Tulips** between two variations on the **Whisper** pattern, and **Viscaria**; Row 2: **Double V**, **Bridgewater**, **Floreat**, **Newlyn**; Row 3: **Nasturtium**, **Football**, **Latona Bouquet**, **Delecia Pansy**, **Diamonds**, and an **Inspiration Knight Errant** *Lotus*.

Inspiration Knight Errant again is seen here on this wall-plaque.

Metallic oxide glazes coupled with very high temperatures gave **Inspiration** its distinctive appearance. The vase with poppies was designed by John Butler, and in front of it is **Clouvre Butterfly** flanked by an **Inspiration Odilon** vase and a stepped vase. (Christies)

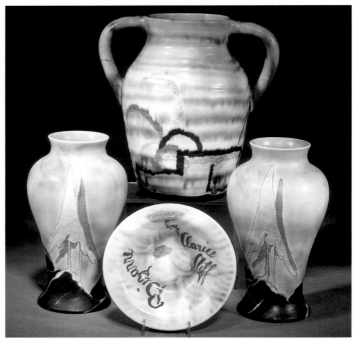

In front of the **Inspiration** twin-handled *Isis* vase are two Meiping vases in **Inspiration Caprice** and an advertising bowl in **Inspiration** reading "Bizarre by Clarice Cliff". (Christies)

Four very varied shapes in **Inspiration Caprice**. *(Christies)*

Three spherical vases, an **Inspiration Clouvre** vase with a metal lid in the background, with a **Double V** vase on the left and a **Berries** vase on the right. (Beverley)

Inspiration Caprice is shown again in the centre of the top row. To the left are **Branch and Squares**, **Oranges and Lemons** and **Erin**, with below them **Sliced Fruit**, **Broth**, **Branch and Squares**, **Appliqué Lugano**, **Berries**, **Passion Fruit**, **Whisper**, **Sunray** and **Apples**, with on the bottom row a stylised tree with slashed orange leaves, two brown vases with red and blue flowers with an example of **Forest Glen** between, and at the end an **Original Delecia**.

Two more rows of vases — **House and Bridge**, **Trees and House**, **Rhodanthe,Sunrise, Gloria Tulip** and **Autumn**, with below a pair of **Delecia Citrus** vases, **Alton**, **Secrets**, a geometric flask vase, **Windbells**, **Country Patina** and **Orange Chintz**.

A variety of shapes showing the **Broth** pattern. (Christies)

Two more striking **Broth** vases. (Christies)

Broth again, this time on a *Yo-yo* vase, with **Honolulu**, **Pastel Autumn** and a *Dutch* Honey-pot. (Beverley)

Orange House on the left and a striped vase with black flowers on the right have in front of them a cafe au lait **Flower and Squares** *Conical* shaker and a Green Cowslip shaker with a metal-topped *Conical* vase behind them, decorated by a narrow band of stylised flowers. (Beverley)

Bowls also come in a wide variety of shapes and patterns, Row 1: **Sandon**, **Lorna** and **Patina Coastal**; Row 2: **Carpet**, an early geometric pattern, **Kelverne**, another geometric pattern; Row 3: **Peter Pan Crocus**, **Rhodanthe**, **Autumn Crocus** and **Double V**. (Christies)

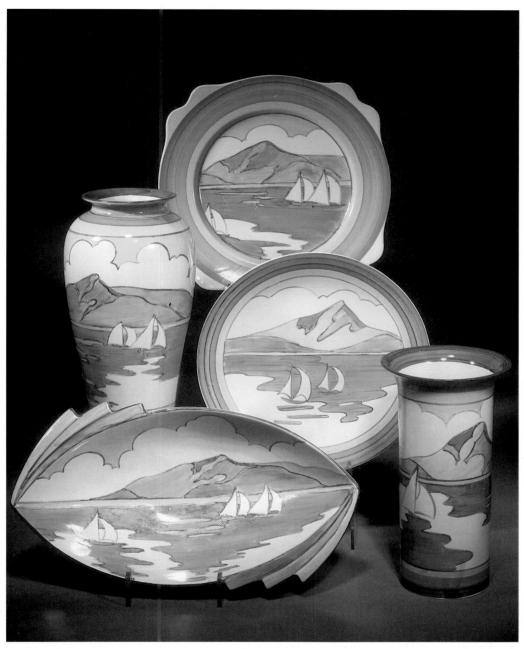

Here, **Gibraltar** displayed on a range of shapes. (Christies)

Gibraltar is in the foreground of these *Conical* shakers, backed by **Orange Autumn**, **Blue Crocus** and **Forest Glen**, with to the rear **Orange Roof Cottage**, **Tulips** and **Blue Firs**. (Christies)

Autumn Crocus, Clarice Cliff's first floral pattern, is also always a favourite, here with a bulbous jug in **Sungleam Crocus**. (Christies)

Two *Farmhouse* examples, with an *Athens* jug in **Red Roofs**. (Christies)

Windbells, a delicate pattern of a curving tree with blue blossom, is shown here on a *Stamford Tea for Two* with a large matching plate . . . . (Christies)

. . . and here on a *Daffodil* shape teapot, vase, single-handed *Lotus* jug and wall-plate.
(Christies)

A selection of bowls, Row 1: **Blue Japan**, **Sunray**, **Stile** and **Trees**; Row 2: **Delecia Citrus**, **Honolulu**, **Persian**, **Summerhouse** and **Broth** and, Row 3: **Oasis**, 7-colour **Trees and House**, **Trees and House** in the usual colourway, **Blue Chintz** and **Oasis**, with Row 4: **Pastel Banding**, **Shark's Teeth**, **Berries** and two early geometric patterns. (Christies)

Sometimes the interior of a bowl was decorated, as in the top row; **House and Bridge**, **Kew**, **Applique Lucerne**, **Red Roofs**, and **Trees and House**, and sometimes the exterior, Row 2: a geometric pattern, **Kew**, **Idyll**, **Blue Firs** and a *Latona* version of **Blue-eyed Marigolds**; Row 3: **Delecia Citrus**, **Solitude**, **Blue Chintz**, **Lorna**, **Gibraltar** and **Sliced Fruit**, and Row 4: **Rudyard**, **Forest Glen**, two **Delecia Pansy** pieces and an unusual version of **Tibetan**, a John Butler design.

63

The large and impressive *Lotus* jugs and *Isis* vases made a perfect surface for any pattern, Row 1: **Rhodanthe**, stylised flowers on orange, **Honolulu**, **Capri**, **Nasturtium**, Row 2: **Forest Glen**, **Cabbage Flower**, **Gloria**, **Hollyrose**, an early geometric, **Trees and House**, Row 3: **Autumn Crocus**, **Aurea**, **Forest Glen**, **Delecia Citrus**, **Latona** with flowerheads and wavy blue lines and **Floreat**. (Christies)

More interesting patterns are shown here; Top: *Autumn Crocus*, *Gloria*, *Orange Double Inspiration V*, *Caprice*, a weeping tree in a landscape, and below, *Sandon*, two strong geometric designs and *Delecia Anemone*. (Christies)

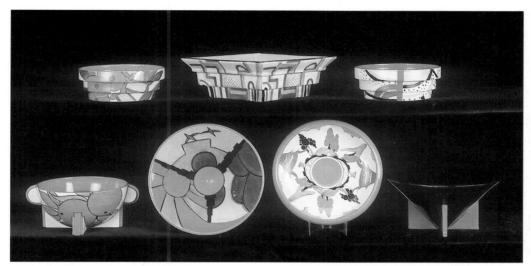

These complicated bowl shapes must have posed problems for the paintresses, Row 1: **Bobbins**, **Tennis** and **Carpet**; Row 2: **Oranges**, **Sunray** and **Kew** with **Yoo Hoo**, a very rare and collectable pattern in black with strong red. (Christies)

Two **Yoo Hoo** coffee pots appear in the middle row here, with to the right a *Lynton* shape decorated with a simple band of leaves, **Nasturtium** and **Appliqué Avignon**. Row 1 has **Delecia Poppy**, **Coral Firs** and **Lily Orange**, while Row 3 shows a *Café au lâit Latona* **Tree**, a geometric pattern, **Gayday**, **Pastel Autumn** and **Orange Chintz**. (Christies)

The **Sliced Fruit** umbrella stand is 69.5cm high. On the left are vases (from top) in **Coral Firs** and **Luxor**, and a **Summerhouse** jardinière, on the right a **Delecia Citrus** bowl, a **Honolulu** vase and a **Rhodanthe** jardinière. The *Golliwog* and *Teddy Bear* bookends are on **Pastel Autumn** bases. (Christies)

The beautiful fantasy landscape, **Moonlight**, looks well on any shape. (Christies)

Orange House (back) and **Honolulu** with in the foreground are also fantasy scenes. (Christies)

The milky *Latona* glaze set off vivid colours. Here, **Latona Bouquet**, with a vase, right, in **Comet**. (Christies)

Autumn, once known as Balloon Trees, comes in a variety of colourways. Here **Orange Autumn**. (Christies)

The vase on the left has a mottled blue and orange ground, possibly experimental, with stylised flowerheads and leaves. The circular vase is **Coral Firs** and the one on the right is **Delecia Pansy**. (Beverley)

Latona again, here as **Latona Dahlia**. (Beverley)

A stunning charger in the **Oranges** pattern, 45.5cm in diameter (Christies)

A group of vases in the **Persian** pattern, produced here on the Inspiration glaze. These Isnic designs were earlier made in traditional colours. (Christies)

Backstamps and other methods of dating

Before very long the Clarice Cliff collector will acquire an instinctive eye for her designs and patterns. A collector can pick out a Clarice Cliff design on sight from among the rest of the goods on sale in a shop or on a stall at an antiques fair, a church fete or jumble sale. Picking up a bargain has been known to happen in the past but as the years go by and Clarice Cliff's name becomes more widely known, this is becoming increasingly difficult. Without even looking at the base of a discovery, the collector can feel fairly sure it is by Clarice Cliff and also can probably say from the shape and pattern whether it is an early piece, an item from the prolific middle period of her work or a later piece. With detailed knowledge of the sequence of shape introduction, one can make an informed guess as to the date of the piece to within a few years. If the pattern is a familiar one, the collector may well know the dates when it was available (setting aside the rather slim possibility that his purchase was a matching, that is, a piece of a pattern decorated especially for a customer who had the misfortune to break part of a set in a discontinued pattern. In the thirties, single items were made to oblige a previous purchaser, quite often several years after the pattern originally brought had been phased out).

For business reasons it was important to be ruthless in cutting out unprofitable lines and some patterns which did not catch the public's fancy survived for only a few months before being weeded out. This, of course, makes them rare today and much sought after by collectors — a kind of posthumous rehabilitation! Apart from long-running favourites like Crocus and Rhodanthe, even successful patterns were only produced for a few years, for they inevitably began to lose popularity and were replaced by something more appealing to current taste.

Shape and pattern, then, will help to date an item but a more accurate guide, as with any pottery, is the backstamp — the trademark or working stamped, printed or impressed on the base.

Many Clarice Cliff items, particularly flat pieces like plates or chargers, do have a date impressed underneath but the collector must be wary, since an impressed date may be misleading, as it is a guide only to the date of manufacture of the pottery and not to the date when the item were decorated. The impressed mark usually gives the month number above the last two digits of the year, along with, in some cases, an embossed shape number, especially on vases.

For the date of decoration an important guide is any additional information given by the wording which was put on at the same time as the pattern itself. This is possible because the form of wording altered from time to time giving us important clues about the date of production. One problematic area here is that the dates of some different marks overlapped, some of them running concurrently for a considerable while. This was because the various ranges had their own marks, sometimes used on very similar stock sold to different retailers. According to Clarice Cliff herself, the Fantasque range for instance, was used as an alternative to the

Bizarre range because 'Bizarre Ware was usually sold to only one customer in a town, so Fantasque was supposed to be a little different and sold to another shop'. The Bizarre backstamp was used from 1928 until 1937 and the Fantasque from 1929 until 1934, to be followed by various Clarice Cliff only backstamps until 1963 when all stamps using her name were discontinued on the sale of the factories to Midwinters.

Initially, the information on the base was handwritten, as no stamps existed and the management were unlikely to have any made until the need for them was proven by a successful sales drive. As a result, 'Bizarre by Clarice Cliff' was at first handwritten, in addition to the underglaze printed factory name, and these were obviously the earliest pieces to reach the shops. The enthusiasm with which they were received clearly justified a rubber stamp to speed up marking and eventually lithographed marks which obviated the possibility of smudging and which could be applied even faster. In fact it is necessary to look very closely to distinguish between the two methods. The lithographs, naturally, were the neater of the two, the rubber stamp generally being used with black ink, though in the early days gilt and pale green inks were also used.

Handpainting continued to be used for adding the pattern name, in script at first and later in block letters, above the main stamp. When it became clear that the pattern, for instance Crocus or Gayday, was likely to continue for some time, lithographs were made for these names as well, and similarly the Inspiration range started off with INSPIRATION handwritten above it. After 1931 handwritten marks of any kind seldom appear, except on the tiny advertising plaques, the backs of which were so small a very fine paintbrush was used, for example, 'FERNDALE by Clarice Cliff', the name of the pattern being in block letters and the rest in script. On these it was essential to identify the letters and the rest in script. On these it was essential to identify the pattern unmistakably, as they were used by the shopkeepers to inform the factory of their customers' latest orders. Collectors often wish it had been the custom to put the pattern names on every piece, but despite advertising boast, 'Look for the name Clarice Cliff on every piece', many items undeniably from the Newport Pottery were sent out without any backstamp at all!

As the Newport order books began to bulge with ever-increasing sales, it became sensible to spread tax liability across the whole operation, and in 1930 'Handpainted by Clarice Cliff, Wilkinson's Pottery, England' joined the 'Handpainted by Clarice Cliff, Newport Pottery, England' used in two stamped sizes from the autumn of 1928. The range name Bizarre was used throughout and Fantasque for a short while in script, then in block letters above Bizarre. Once lithography was introduced, Fantasque appeared alone again and Bizarre as a lithograph credited, 'Newport' until 1934.

The Biarritz range, introduced by 1933, had its own distinguishing mark. This sometimes had a Clarice Cliff mark added to it as well, and sometimes a Bizarre mark too. It seems there were hardly any strict rules about backstamps. Sometimes even the base of a tea cup will carry a wealth of contradictory information whilst a large item like a meat dish carries no identifying marks at all!

From this it can be seen that even with all three strands of information — shape, pattern and backstamp — it is difficult to date any item with absolute certainty, though a fairly accurate idea can be obtained in this way. The best method of all is to date the piece by provenance — if it is being purchased from the original owner, an exact date is sometimes given:

'It was bought for us for our wedding in 1932 . . .'

'I saved up out of my first few months' wages for it in 1934 . . .'

'My Mother bought it for me to put in my bottom drawer in 1935 when I was eighteen . . .'

'I got into trouble for breaking the other two plates in 1937 when my mother had only just had that set for her fortieth birthday.'

This is the hard evidence that authenticates the age of a new acquisition, gives it considerable human interest and links today's collector with the time when the china shops had shelves full of the very latest Clarice Cliff designs.

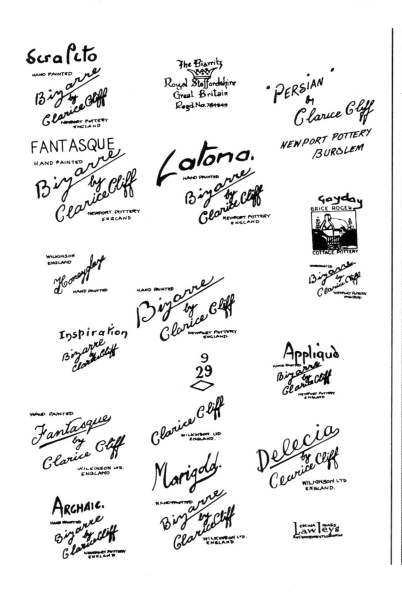

Some examples of Clarice Cliff backstamps

Shape Guide

Conical

Bonjour

Stamford

Trieste

Lynton

Athens

Snail

Conical

Bonjour

Daffodil

Lynton

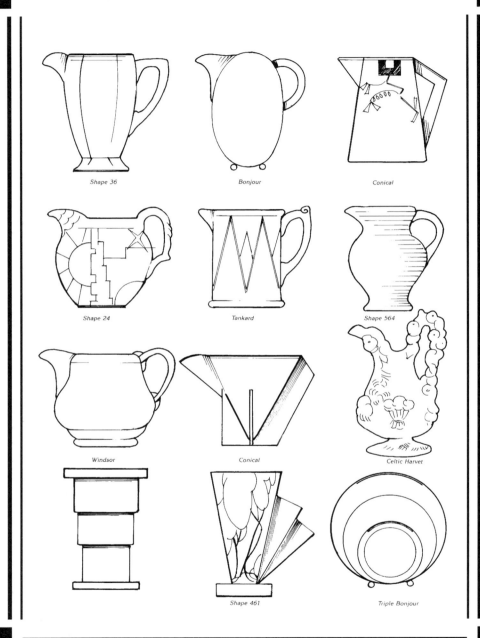

Shape 36

Bonjour

Conical

Shape 24

Tankard

Shape 564

Windsor

Conical

Celtic Harvet

Shape 461

Triple Bonjour

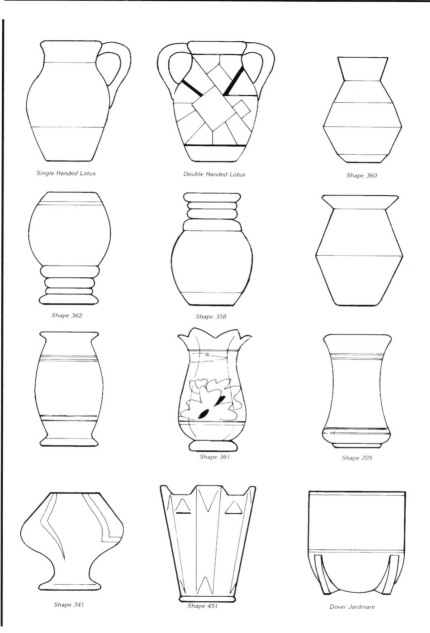

Single Handed Lotus

Double Handed Lotus

Shape 360

Shape 362

Shape 358

Shape 341

Shape 361

Shape 205

Shape 451

Dover Jardinare

Shape 269

Shape 196

Isis

Shape 370

Meiping

Stamford

Handled Jug

Conical

Yo-Yo Vase

Stamford

Finned Stamford

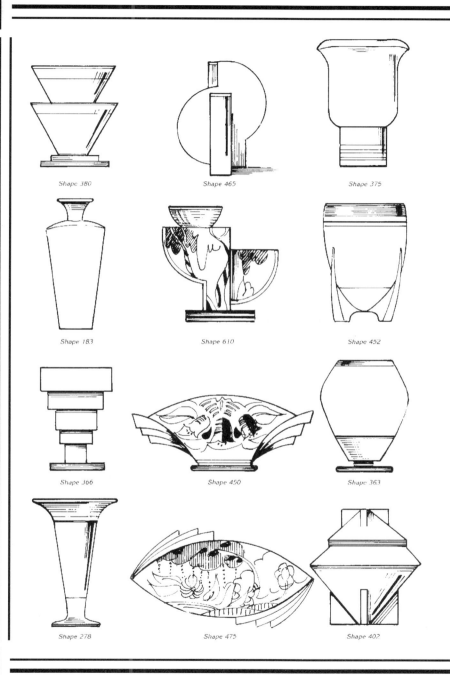

Shape 380

Shape 465

Shape 375

Shape 183

Shape 610

Shape 452

Shape 366

Shape 450

Shape 363

Shape 278

Shape 475

Shape 402

Pattern Names Old and New

Not all the original Clarice Cliff pattern names have been handed down to us. The safest and easiest way to identify a pattern is when the name is handwritten or printed by means of a transfer on the base of the ware itself. Then there is no room for doubt. Some patterns can similarly be identified from the Newport Pottery pattern books held in the Wilkinson's archives at Hanley Library, while others appear in contemporary advertisements to be found in the *Pottery Gazette and Glass Trades Review* (which is available there too). Other patterns have been named from memory by the surviving paintresses who were familiar with them from working for Clarice Cliff and Colley Shorter, and these have been recorded in the review of the Clarice Cliff Collectors Club and elsewhere.

For the convenience of collectors, appropriate pattern names have been coined for unidentified patterns and some of these have passed into common usage (to such an extent that it is only with an effort that a collector remembers the name he is using is not in fact the original name by which the pattern was known, but one bestowed on it half a century later).

A further complication is that different names were used for the various colourways of a pattern. For instance, the Honolulu pattern before it was finally identified was usually called Zebra Trees or Tiger Trees by collectors, while the original name of the blue colourway of this pattern was **Rudyard**.

The early geometric patterns were regular in their design and there is no mistaking their bold simplicity. Later, patterns appeared which were abstract in character, featuring irregular shapes which sometimes suggest a pictorial effect like a stylised landscape, or else which appear to be patterns used simply for the sake of achieving an all-over effect, as in the pattern known to collectors as Tennis.

Similarly, banding was at first used boldly, with wide bands of contrasting colours covering the item completely. Later, fine banding, requiring considerable skill to apply, was also used, sometimes to provide a textured background on top of which floral or landscape motifs were added. **Capri** is an example of this, and **Liberty** is an example of banding, thick or thin, used simply as a quick and easy method of rapid decoration when a rush order was received and there was no time available for more elaborate patterns. There are times in all jobs when demand outstrips supply and tricks of the trade are needed to make up the shortfall quickly and economically. Clever colour combinations prevented the short cuts from looking too obvious. A speedy cover-up, orange, yellow and black banding, is one which positively sings out, for its brightness, yet it could have been applied at top speed by a skilled bander.

In a similar way, as orders poured in and the Newport workshops were stretched to their limit, the use of transfers was tried to speed up the outlining, which was then filled in by hand and combined with hand-painted banding. **Solomon's Seal** was perhaps the most successful example of this, but in general it was not popular with customers, who preferred the totally hand-painted look.

Towards the end of the Thirties, however, coloured lithography was used for conventional country scenes, with just a touch of banding done by hand. These examples are not eagerly sought by collectors even though they compare favourably with lithographic decoration produced by other firms.

A more imaginative short-cut was the application on tableware of shoulder patterns, that is, a slice of a popular pattern hand-painted on each item of a large dinner or tea service, so that set out on a dining table a bright attractive effect was produced, especially when it was combined as it sometimes was with hand-embroidered table-napkins matching the pattern and with a large wall-plaque displayed nearby with the complete pattern on it. Another speedy method of decoration was to reduce the pattern to a small rectangle which was then applied like a stamp on one corner of every piece, so that the chosen pattern was displayed in a miniaturised version. This, too, could be very attractive.

Clarice Cliff must have realised that to follow up the success of the original Bizarre Ware, she needed something colourful and exciting, but it had to be something easy to paint, for her girls had not at that time acquired the expertise for complicated brushwork. In the autumn of 1928 she came up with **Crocus** and was at once on to a winner. This was to outstrip all other patterns in popularity and today still has the most immediate and recognisable appeal. It had the added advantage of being simple to apply in a variety of colourways, and pastel **Spring Crocus** came a close second to the original purple, orange and dark blue of **Autumn Crocus**. **Sungleam** – orange and yellow flowers only – was like a ray of sunshine, and **Blue Crocus** had its admirers, but today it is Purple Crocus which is gasped over and envied. Paradoxically, it was less popular in the 1930s than in the other colourways of **Crocus** and so it is even rarer and more desirable as an addition to a collection.

Another popular pattern, dating from 1929, was **Ravel,** which combines stylised flowers and leaves with angular motifs to give an oriental effect. The colours are attractive – dark green, orange and black on a Honeyglaze background- and there is a hint of sophistication in its restraint. Perhaps Clarice had in mind customers for whom **Crocus**, in its rainbow of colours was too naive, too "folk-art". Certainly the rare maroon and dark blue colourway of **Ravel**, known as **Brunella**, is almost sombre in comparison with the rest of the factory's output at the time, while the dark blue and orange colourway, its name unknown, is even more rare. **Cherry**, one of Clarice's combinations of natural shapes with a geometric background, also used darker colours but in such a way as to give a light impression, whilst fans of Clarice's original uninhibited colourful palette were well catered for with more adventurous patterns. She was still using brilliant orange, green and blue in **Broth**, **Lily** and **Umbrellas & Rain**, while **Sunray** is a triumph of complicated stylisation. Known to collectors also as *Night & Day*, it features skyscrapers, bridges, stars, clouds and the sun's rays fitting together in a jigsaw of clashing colours.

The following year, 1930, saw the arrival on the scene of **Gayday,** a pattern rich in red, blue and orange asters. It was complemented by **Sungay**, an alternative colourway which used yellow, green and bright blue. Not as long-lived as **Crocus**, being produced primarily between 1930 and 1934, it is also a pattern often found in a shabby condition, for the on-glaze blue has seldom worn well and this is a point worth watching when a purchase is under consideration. **Gayday** was made in considerable quantity and it is worth watching out for a good specimen.

Not so easy to find, and in some ways more attractive, with its multicoloured, all-over effect, is **Berries**, another 1930s pattern which went out of production the following year. **Melon**, once called *Picasso Fruit* because of its Cubist influence, is an outstanding example of Clarice's skill in blending colour and style in a pattern adaptable to every available size. It looks well on everything from a Lotus jug to an egg-cup. Much rarer than either of these, though, is *Butterfly*, which may or may not be its original name. Against a background of orange, yellow and beige stripes, large butterflies in red, black, blue and green are painted with bold strokes. These cut across the piece uncompromisingly when the shape of the ware demands it.

One evening, early in her career, it is said, Clarice Cliff stayed behind after the other girls had gone home, and painted a butterfly on a piece of pottery left lying on a bench. This caught the eye of Jack Walker, the Decorating Manager, who showed it to Colley Shorter, his brother-in-law, thus setting in train all that was to follow. Perhaps the *Butterfly* pattern of 1930 was a tribute to that earlier butterfly, painted so casually and which was yet so crucial, not only to her own future but to that of the whole factory, for there is no doubt at all that it was Clarice Cliff's success that kept her employers ahead in the race for orders.

By now landscapes had joined the fruit and flowers in the pattern books as the Bizarre Girls gained greater skill in brush control and were able to paint quite complicated patterns at high speed. **Trees & House**, sometimes called *Alpine*, featured one of the many cottages Clarice Cliff loved to include in her designs, flanked by trees and nestling among hills. **Gibraltar**, a popular seascape in mainly pastel colours included the Rock of Gibraltar and though a good seller in its day is now very rare and collectable. **Red Roofs** included huge orange flowers on the reverse and orange flowers climbing up the walls of the red-roofed cottage, while **Orange Roof Cottage** is easily recognisable by the brown bridge arching across the centre of the picture and by the distinctive black banding in contrast to the red, yellow, green and blue of the main picture. **House & Bridge**, in which the colours are red, yellow, orange and black, was chosen for the dust-wrapper of Peter Wentworth-Sheilds and Kay Johnson's book, *Clarice Cliff,* published by L'Odeon in 1976, and thus became known as the "Cover of the Book" pattern, one which collectors are particularly keen to have in their collections. In this, too, there is a bridge, but it is offset to the left, the little cluster of buildings being to the right, with the tree trunk slicing boldly across the centre.

In **Secrets**, said to be one of Clarice's own favourites, the cottages are tucked away almost out of sight among the folds of the landscape, while in **Autumn** (previously called Balloon Trees because of the trees twisting sinuously across the centre with clumps of massed foliage near the top) and in **Coral Firs** and **Blue Firs**, its other colourway, it is the trees which dominate the whole design. Like Melon, Autumn was highly successful in pastel colourways as well as in its original glowing primary colours and was adapted to every shape, including some very rare ones. Alongside the landscapes, new flowers bloomed, including **Floreat**, one featuring geometrically-styled marigolds. **Gardenia** is a pattern with bold orange, blue and purple flowers with green and black leaves, and **Marguerite** had daisy-like flowers moulded on to the surface of the ware and painted blue and pink.

Poplar gained its name from the two poplar trees combined with a cottage and large flowers, but perhaps the most apt name was **Chintz**, for an all-over pattern of waterlilies, so heavily stylised that the design was nicknamed *Poached Egg* by early collectors. Available in blue, green and orange colourways, it would have been equally at home as a fabric design as on pottery.

To many, though, the most interesting pattern of those first years was **Delecia**, which began simply as an adventurous abstract design, by letting thinned paint drip freely to produce random colour combinations with startling results. Later, bands of fruit or flowers were added to contrast with the dripping below, and the effect of the skillfully-painted decoration with the **Delecia** background was subtle and attractive, the fruit or flowers being treated more realistically than in the earlier, stylised patterns.

By now the paintresses had developed enough skill and experience to tackle patterns demanding more complex techniques, such as etching. This is not meant in the usual sense of the word, for in the pottery industry it is applied to a method of blending brushstrokes of colour to create a shaded effect. This was used for Clarice's **Rhodanthe** pattern, in oranges and browns, and its later colourways, the pink **Viscaria** and the green **Aurea**. In all three, large flowers are held up near the top of the ware by long, sinuous stems, their roots hidden by more flower heads set on meandering grassy banks. Particularly successful on the rectangular *Biarritz* plates, this was a very popular design which perhaps indicates that public taste was turning to more subdued colour combinations. Certainly about this time Clarice Cliff began to develop her **My Garden** range of vases, bowls and jugs in which moulded garlands of brightly coloured flowers decorated the base or the handle, with body colours in tasteful shades of beige, green, reddish brown or, more rarely, black, as well as in matt or glazed mushroom. In January, 1934, the firm had advertised in a horticultural magazine called "My Garden", so perhaps this was the inspiration for the range name. Headed, "Designed by a lover of flowers for flower lovers", the advertisement goes on, "Miss Clarice Cliff loves flowers and knows how to provide settings for them. Her latest vases and bowls are charming in their originality of design and colour, and are eminently practical." It is easy to forget, now Clarice's pottery is so collectable, that practicality was a strong selling point, and all the wares were made for everyday use.

It was also made to sell, and the prevailing tastes had to be given due consideration. Perhaps this is why Clarice so often adapted established designs to bring them into line with current trends. An instance of this is **Tulips**, a pretty landscape incorporating a cottage, a balloon tree and a row of the flowers that gave it its name. With the cottage removed and a crinoline lady substituted, it became **Idyll.** Clearly this was successful, as a variety of crinoline ladies then made their appearance, usually in gardens, sometimes with cottages, sometimes without.

The crinoline lady was a popular motif of the day and appeared on pottery, firescreens, tablemats and on embroidered traycloths and cushions. Few, however, will have had patches of orange and black incorporated into the design, along with the conventional pastel blues and pinks! Another stunning pattern was **Forest Glen**, in which Clarice combined her cottage-and-tree motif with a **Delecia** sky in bold reds, browns and greys, to startling effect, so that the cottage appears against a stormy, bloodshot sky. It was also produced in a blue colourway called **Newlyn**.

This was to be one of the last of Clarice's landscapes, along with **Trallee**, which utilised the **Rhodanthe** etching technique to produce a large, thatched cottage with a garden full of large orange and yellow flowers. Clarice also took the moulding technique of the **My Garden** range much further, to produce **Celtic Harvest**, in which wheat sheaves are moulded against a basket weave background, and clumps of brightly coloured fruit and flowers are used as handles and knobs.Sometimes made with chrome lids and rims, this was not a pattern which has appealed strongly to collectors in the past, but there is a lot to be said for the exuberance of the teapots and pitchers with their riotously encrusted handles and pot bellied shapes. One isolated piece of **Celtic Harvest** may be considered to be the product of Clarice Cliff on an off-day, but seen as a group the range has considerable beauty all of its own.

As well as the patterns which can be fitted into the firm's output by name and date, there remain many for which there is little information. One such is the extremely rare pattern. Moselle, the name being inscribed on the base but without any clues as to its original date. It is a design outlined strongly in black and with red curliques, consisting of stylised flower-heads in blue, orange, green, red and black, with no echoes of any other pattern to suggest when it was produced. On the other hand, a pattern given the name *Bobbins*, which has circular orange and red flowers and leaves with orange, red and yellow cotton-reel shapes also has light brown banding, suggesting an early Thirties date. Another pattern, which has blue, orange, yellow and black poached-egg type flowers on a black background is included in the 1929 pattern book but again without a name, now called 'Garland'.

Some patterns were only given names after they had been in production for some time. There are inevitably many others for which precise information may never be known. After all, Clarice Cliff was one of the most prolific pottery designers of all times – it has been suggested that early in her career she was for several years turning out up to twenty-seven new designs every week, the ultimate total being said to be over two thousand! No wonder, then. that mysteries remain, and perhaps always will. It is the price collectors pay for the outstanding creativity and versatility of Clarice Cliff.

Decorating Techniques

In addition to the design and testing of new patterns and shapes which never stopped during the production and marketing of established lines, much of Clarice Cliff's time was taken up in experimenting with new decorating techniques, not all of them it must be said, equally successful. Every year saw at least one new surface texture introduced, always the end product of weeks of testing and discussion. These innovations were born out of the awareness of Colley Shorter and Clarice herself for the need to give the buying public novelty and variety.

The launch of Bizarre Ware had been achieved in a blaze of publicity, and they knew that in order to maintain the momentum it was essential to catch the fickle attention of their customers by announcing new discoveries and fresh ideas in pottery production. So pressing was this need that even when the special effects were tricky to produce, as long as they seemed likely to intrigue and attract potential purchasers, they were offered as the very latest sensation, backed up by all the media hype and marketing expertise Colley Shorter could build into it.

This is not to say that many of the special decorating techniques were not genuinely interesting, unusual and effective. The **Inspiration** range especially was a true innovation, in which the use of a mixture of metallic oxide glazes produced superb results in deep rich blues, turquoises, pinks and pale mauves. To some degree this was an extension of the work done at Wilkinson's on art pottery glazes before Bizarre Ware was started, work which, in fact, involved the young Clarice Cliff herself as a gilder. **Inspiration** proved extremely difficult to fire, as the thin glaze tended to run down the ware, and while this produced an attractive end result it also had the unfortunate effect of gluing the pottery to the kiln furniture on which it rested, This in turn meant that upon removal from the kiln the trimmers had to go through a time consuming process of separating them and smoothing off the raw edges, during which either the pottery or the props could easily be damaged.

Though marketed with much romantic advertising as being the true Scarab blue, (a long lost secret from Ancient Egypt) **Inspiration** was unpopular with the paintresses as the rough surface made their fingers sore. It was expensive to produce and expensive to buy. Being made in limited quantities it was sold at prices much higher than the humble **Crocus**, for instance. Rarely found, it remains expensive today and no-one could deny the beauty of its brilliant colours, although not everybody likes the rather crude patterns (such as **Knight Errant**, featuring a knight in armour before a medieval castle) preferring the more abstract effects which certainly are very striking.

Inspiration began in 1929, when Clarice Cliff was heavily involved in organising the early rush orders for Bizarre Ware, so she may have had less to do with its development than she did with the other, less hazardous special glaze of that year, **Latona**, a milky glaze combined with a range of specially designed floral patterns, depending for their effect on large areas of solid colour. This combination of an eggshell finish with eye-catching colour gave **Latona** a subtle brilliance that set it apart from the rest of the Bizarre range. "Latona gives the full glory of modern colouring on beautiful, satiny, matt glazes of varying tones," claimed the advertisements, hoping to convince the customers they couldn't live without it. Equally novel was the **Applique** range which followed it in 1930, a sumptuous style of all over hand-painting in luscious colours which showed Clarice at her daring best. It required great skill as it was painted without an outline and in the earlier examples no Honeyglaze was allowed to show through. These are regarded as among the most successful of all of Clarice Cliff's work. They have a stunning directness with red, black, orange, green and blue somehow harmonising in scenes reminiscent of a book of fairy tales – castles, gardens, bridges, wind and watermills, ornamental birds and flowers and even a gypsy caravan being among the motifs. Like **Inspiration** (though for different reasons), **Applique** was time consuming to produce and therefore expensive. Though produced for several years it was never made in large quantities and so today is difficult to find except at high prices.

As the Bizarre range expanded, new techniques were tried which could be used in conjunction with existing patterns. One such was *Cafe au Lait*, a method of applying paint with a sponge to produce a stippled surface to which a pattern could be added, or which could be applied over certain parts of a pattern, giving an interesting variety of surface. Sometimes areas were left free for the pattern, sometimes the pattern was added on top, allowing great flexibility of application. Not only the obvious coffee colour was used but a number of others including yellow, blue and green. Similar was *Nuage*, also applied with a sponge but using thickened paint to create a textured surface, and involving two areas of stippling in different colours with a hand of fruit or flowers between them. Less successful than either of these was *Damask Rose*. As its name implies, it had a light pinky beige glaze which was hard to apply and which was used, appropriately enough, with floral patterns. This was phased out after less than a year. Meanwhile, **Patina** had been created, which had a more adventurous effect caused by splattering 'slip' (liquid clay) coloured either grey or pink, on the surface of the ware to give it a roughened texture, which was then glazed before the application of the pattern. These were specially designed to be simple to apply on the uneven areas. Possibly because it lacked the smoothness usually associated with pottery it was not popular and little was made, no doubt to the relief of the paintresses for whom it must have made life difficult.

In contrast to the different surfaces created by these various techniques, **Goldstone** went further, for a different type of clay was used for the pottery, combined with a speckled surface resulting from the mixing of a kind of metallic dust in the glaze. There is something curiously modern about the result, which has a distinct resemblance to hand-thrown studio pottery of the 1980s. The minimum of decoration was used, occasionally with touches of gold lining to brighten up the plain brown surface. **Goldstone** pieces are wafer thin and when chipped the clay has a friable, crumbly look. The appearance of the range is in complete contrast to the rest of Clarice Cliff's work, so much so that it frequently goes unrecognised as her work until her signature is seen on the base. This is true also of the very rare oriental-type glaze in grey-green, which we have called 'Celadon', so far found only undecorated, and the similar **Kang**, a blue-grey glaze under which moulded bosses provide decoration.

By this time, around 1935, the whole situation was changing for Clarice Cliff and in future she was to concentrate her efforts on pottery with more mass appeal than on her earlier, highly original, experiments – which had met with mixed success and which, in any case, would only appeal to a limited clientele. The changing economic climate meant that the heady days of Bizarre and Fantasque were over. In future, Clarice would play it safe, relying on a mushroom glaze with pretty touches of pink and blue, or warm autumnal colours on simple sprays of leaves, attractive in their own way, perhaps, but insipid when compared with the vigour of her early exuberant palette. Her experimental years, however, left behind a rich legacy, and **Inspiration**, **Applique**, **Latona** and **Patina** will always be names to conjure with for collectors of her work.

Pattern Index and Dates

c=Date of discontinuation approximate

Note:

Numerals in brackets indicate probable price range as in the price guide, but must regarded as flexible, many other factors besides pattern being likely to affect price. Patterns enclosed within " " are popular names, assigned by dealers/collectors where no official pattern name exists.

Name	Price Range	Dates	Page
Alton	(2)	1933-1934	56
Amberose	(2)	1933-1934	29
Apples	(2/3)	1931-1932	56
Applique Avignon	(3)	1930-1931	37,39,48,65
Applique Caravan	(3)	1930-c1931	47
Applique Lucerne	(3)	1930-1932/3	41,52,63
Applique Lugano	(3)	1930-1932	41,56
Applique Palermo	(3)	1930-1931	43
Applqiue Red Tree	(3)	1930	23,41
Applique Windmill	(3)	1930-1931	39
Aurea	(1)	1935-1937	29,64
Autumn	(2/3)	1930-1934	22,32,35,42,52,56
Orange	(2/3)	1932 onwards	35,46,60 69
Pastel	(2/3)	1933 onwards	32,34,35,57,65,66
Autumn Crocus or Original Crocus	(1)	1928-1963 (except war years)	28,29,32,35,58,60,64
Berries	(2)	1930-1931	43,55,56,63
Blue Chintz	(2)	1932-c1933	29,29,32,35,63
Blue Crocus	(2)	1935	27,60
Blue Firs	(2)	1933-1936	19,20,60,63
Blue Japan	(2)	1937	35,63
Blue Ribbon	(2)	1932	35
"Blue W"	(3)	1929-1930	32,52,53
"Bobbins"	(2)	1931-1932	65
"Branch and Squares"	(2)	1930	35,56
Bridgewater	(2)	1934	32,53
Broth	(2/3)	1929-1930	56,57,63
"Butterfly"	(2/3)	1929-1930	39
"Cabbage Flower"	(2)	1934	64
Capri	(1)	1933-1934	27,64

Name	Price Range	Dates	Page
"Carpet"	(2/3)	1930	58,65
"Circle Tree"	(2/3)	1929-1930	27,28,47
"Comet"	(3)	1930	68
"Coral Firs"	(2)	1933-1936	20,29,35,65,66,70
Crayon Scenes (6 variations)	(1)	1934	35
"Cubes"	(2/3)	1929	48
Delecia Anemone	(2)	1933-1934	64
Delecia Citrus	(2)	1932-1933	27,29,31,35,48,56, 63,64,66
Delecia Daisy	(2)	1933-1934	29
Delecia Pansy	(2)	1933-1934	28,29,53,63,70
Delecia Poppy	(2)	1933-1934	35,65
Devon	(2/3)	1933	43,52
"Diamonds"	(2/3)	1929	53
"Double V"	(3)	1929	28,35,53,55,58,64
Erin	(2)	1933-1934	56
Etna	(3)	1931-1932	23
Farmhouse	(2)	1931-1932	60
Floreat	(2)	1930	53,64
Floral Nuage	(2)	1931	28
"Flowers and Squares"	(2)	1930	58
"Football"	(2/3)	1929-1930	51,53
Forest Glen	(2)	1936-1937	28,29,32,40,42,56, 60,63,64
Gardenia	(2)	1931-1932	28,35
"Garland"	(1)	1929	32
Gayday	(1)	1930-1934	65
Gibraltar	(2)	1931-1932	21,31,59,60,63
Gloria	(2)	1930-1931	64
Gloria Tulip	(2)	1930-1931	56
Green Cowslip	(2)	1933-1934	58
Hollyrose	(2)	1932	64
Honolulu	(2)	1933-1934	32,44,57,63,64,66,68
House and Bridge	(2)	1931-1933	35,56,63
Idyll	(3)	1931-1935	28,29,44,45,46,63
Inspiration Caprice	(3)	1929-1931	54,55,56,64
Inspiration Clouvre Butterfly	(3)	1930-1931	54,55
Inspiration Knight Errant	(3)	1930-1931	53,54

Name	Price Range	Dates	Page
Kelverne	(2)	1936	29,32,53,58
Kew	(2)	1932-1933	63,65
Latona (glaze used)	(3)	1929-1931	
Latona "Blue-eyed Marigolds"	(3)	1930	63
Latona "Bouquet"	(3)	1930	53,68
Latona Dahlia	(3)	1930-1931	70
Latona "Tree"	(3)	1929-1930	35,65
Latona "Flowerheads"	(3)	1929	64
Lily Orange	(2)	1929-1930	65
Limberlost	(2/3)	1932	35
Lorna	(2)	1936	58,63
Luxor	(2/3)	1929-1930	22,26,42,66
Lydiat	(2)	1933	32
Marguerite	(2)	1932-1933	29
May Avenue	(3)	1932-1933	17
Melon	(2/3)	1930-1933	22,28,31,35,50
Moonlight	(2/3)	1932-1933	67
Nasturtium	(2)	1932-c1933	29,31,53,64,65
Newlyn	(2)	1935-1936	40,53
Oasis	(2/3)	1933	63
Orange Chintz	(2)	1932-1933	29,31,56,65
Orange House	(2)	1930	48,58,68
Orange Roof Cottage	(2)	1932-c1933	32,60
Oranges	(2)	1930-1931	28,29,65,71
Oranges and Lemons	(2)	1931-1932	31,56
Original Delecia	(2)	1930-1931	32,56
Passion Fruit	(1)	1936	56
Patina "Coastal"	(2)	1932-1933	58
Patina "Country"	(2)	1932-1933	56
Patina "Tree"	(2)	1932-1933	31
Persian 2	(3)	1930-1931	63,72
Peter Pan Crocus	(1)	1930-1931	28,58
Pink Roof Cottage	(2)	1932-1933	21
"Pink Tree"	(2)	1935	28
Poplar	(2)	1932	50
"Propeller"	(3)	1931	21,27

Name	Price Range	Dates	Page
"Red Flower"	(2)	1930	48
Red Gardenia	(2/3)	1930-1932	36
Red Roofs	(2)	1931	30,31,49,60,63
Rhodanthe	(1)	1934-1941 and postwar	28,29,32,56,58,64,66
Rudyard	(2)	1933-1934	28,63
Sandon	(2)	1935	58,64
Secrets	(2)	1933-1937	28,29,52,56
"Sharks Teeth"	(2)	1930	63
"Sliced Circle"	(2/3)	1930	21
"Sliced Fruit"	(2)	1930	56,63,66
Solitude	(2/3)	1933	27,28,63
Solomon's Seal	(1)	1930	24
Stile and Trees	(1)	1937	63
Summerhouse	(2)	1931-1933	22,27,32,43,63,66
"Sunburst"	(2)	1930	26,38
Sungleam Crocus	(1)	1928	27,60
Sunray	(2/3)	1929-1930	18,23,39,53,56,63,65
"Sunrise"	(2)	1929-c1930	26,43,56
Sunshine	(1)	1930-1931	29
"Swirls"	(2)	1930	27,31
"Tennis"	(2/3)	1931	52,65
Trallee	(2)	1935-1936	35
Trees and House	(2)	1929-1931	28,31,32,42,48,56, 63,64
"Tulip and Leaves"	(2)	1930	28
Tulips	(2)	1934-1935	23,53,60
Viscaria	(1)	1934-1936	28,53
"Wax Flower"	(2)	1930	48
"Whisper"	(2)	1928-1929	53,56
Windbells	(2)	1933-1934	44,56,61,62
"Yoo Hoo"	(2/3)	1930-1931	65

The Clarice Cliff Collectors Club

The Clarice Cliff Collectors Club was formed by Leonard R. Griffin in 1982, and since then has researched much original material on both the pottery and Clarice's life story. With American collector Louis Meisel, Len has produced the book, Clarice Cliff & The Bizarre Affair which has 60 colour plates and is published in Great Britain by Thames and Hudson. The club continues to research both the pottery and Clarice's life and holds meetings for members each year, where new material is shown, and members have a chance to meet some of the original paintresses, Bizarre girls, all of whom are now in their seventies.

The Clarice Cliff Collectors Club can be contacted through the Chairman:
Leonard R. Griffin
Fantasque House
Tennis Drive
The Park
Nottingham NG7 1AE

Auction Trends and Price Guide

It is interesting to compare the highspots, in terms of prices paid (including premiums) at the Clarice Cliff specialist sales held at major auction houses like Christie's South Kensington Limited, over recent years. A word of caution, applying to all auctions, however, is necessary, as the auction room atmosphere may well bring out hidden rivalries, leading to artificially high prices as two or more bidders get locked into a battle for one item. The resulting tension encourages higher and higher bids, and the final purchase price may well be far more than the piece could have realised in calmer circumstances. Also the catalogue illustrations inevitably tend to focus on certain lots to the disadvantage of others, since not every lot can be illustrated. An eye-catching cover can be made by selecting a group of spectacular items which then become the most talked about and sought after pieces in the sale.

For instance, the cover of Christie's catalogue for the sale in March, 1989, carried a photograph of items in the **Sunray** pattern, and these certainly attracted very good bids – a jardinière over £3500/$5600, a **Tea for Two** nearly £3000/$4800, but six Laura Knight **Circus** plates in an usual colourway reached £11000/$17600, as against an estimate of £1000-£1500/$1600-$2400, a **May Avenue** vase realised over £6000/$9600 and an **Inspiration** coffee service with gilt interiors £5000/$8000 plus, so other patterns also held their own. In November the same year the catalogue cover featured Appliqué items in dazzling array – there had been no Appliqué in the previous sale. Now an **Appliqué Lugano** *Conical* jug, despite a hairline crack to the rim, reached close to £4000/$6400, and a 23cm plate in **Appliqué Windmill** was more than £4000/$6400. Once more, **May Avenue** remained popular at nearly £2500/$4000 for a *Daffodil* jug, and the work that had been produced for Clarice Cliff by famous artists of the day was still attracting high bids – £8500/$13600 for a set of beer pitcher and six tankards by Dame Laura Knight and over £7000/$11200 for a matching circular dish.

In the October sale of the following year a mixture of highly desirable items were shown on the front cover, including **Sunray**, **Appliqué** and **Luxor**, with an array of *Conical* shakers, ranging from **Crocus** to **May Avenue** on the back cover, (kept till last, the **May Avenue** shaker fetched almost £2000/$3200). This time, however, no doubt due to the prevailing economic climate, prices did not rise so high, though an **Appliqué Caravan** plate brought over £2000/$3200 and a Laura Knight **Circus** teapot £2500/$4000. In November 1991, the Appliqué range continued to rise steadily, a 18cm vase in **Appliqué Avignon** going for £3500/$5600 while others in the range fetched £1300/$2100, £1500/$2400 and £1700/$2700, but other patterns were popular too, especially at this time **Carpet**, a double-handed *Lotus* jug being £2500/$4000, while the price for a single-handled **Sunray** *Lotus* jug was £2200/$3500 and for a single-handled **Tennis Lotus** jug £1700/$2700. Apart from these top prices, overall this was again a less expensive auction, and it was not till November 1992 that an **Appliqué Blue Lugano** 31cm vase soared to £7000/$11200, an all-time high for a single item, with **Latona Red Roses**, **Sunray** and **Football** vases all between £2000-£3000/$3200-$4800. The trend continued the following year with an **Appliqué Avignon** coffee service fetching £3850/$6200, an **Appliqué Blue Lucerne** *Isis* vase being the same price, an **Appliqué Windmill** vase £2750/$4400, the same as an **Inspiration Persian** double *Yo-yo* vase, and an **Appliqué Caravan** plate just below this at £2420/$3900. In 1991 "Age of Jazz" figures had taken around £2000/$3200 each but in two years they had doubled – £4620/$7400 for two musicians (one piece) and £3740/$6000 for a dancing couple. The auction in November 1994 brought another record high – £12100/$19400 for an **Etna** charger. Other high prices were £4400/$7040 given for a **"Blue W"** single-handled *Lotus* jug, around £3000/$4800 each for chargers in **Clouvre**, **Oranges** and **Solitude** and around £2000/$3200 each for **Appliqué Caravan** vases and an **Appliqué Lucerne** plate.

Prices overall at this sale were high, especially for **Appliqué** *Athens* jugs in **Red Tree** and **Palermo** being £1320/$2100 each, while as always **May Avenue** was popular, a *Conical* beaker going for £1100/$1760 and a restored biscuit barrel for £990/$1580. Latona did well, too, a **Latona Orange Dahlia** vase costing £1540/$2560 and a single-handled **Latona Bouquet** *Lotus* jug £1320/$2100. The sale in April 1995, though in most cases the estimates could be said to be on the low side, nevertheless produced some spectacular results, a **Sliced Circle** doubled-handled *Lotus* jug reaching £4500/$7200, an **Appliqué Blue Lugano** *Conical* coffee pot selling for £2250/$3600, and a **Red Trees and House** 45cm charger £4275/$6840, while a charger designed by Dame Laura Knight which was inspired by the artist's ballerina series, also 45cm, went for a staggering £6187/$9900. On the whole, prices were high, **Windbells** fetching top-estimate bids in many cases, with **Limberlost** and **Secrets** also popular patterns. Now that the economy is said to be recovering, it will be interesting to see what new highspots are reached at Christie's regular Clarice Cliff sales and similar ones being started elsewhere. No doubt, as usual, some items will attract maximum attention, but experience shows there are also always some reasonable buys and even the occasional bargain for the collector able to keep his head and make appropriate bids, unmoved by the sometimes hectic atmosphere around him.

Price and Pattern Guide

In preparing or using a price guide for Clarice Cliff pottery, it must be borne in mind that prices are bound to vary in accordance with collecting trends, with the economic climate, with regional disparities, and above all with different overheads and profit margins. However, what might be called the "desirability factor" remains surprisingly constant, so that if one item is worth today twice as much as another item, the proportion of the prices is likely to remain constant. Pattern, shape and condition are the three factors which must be taken into consideration, with perfect pieces being assumed in this guide.

That said, the only real guide as to the value or worth of a particular piece is the amount that the collector is prepared to spend. The existence of gaps in a collection will, of course, be a spur to the collector to make further purchases, while the price he is asked to pay will depend to a large extent on the rarity of the piece or pieces he has in mind – and how fashionable the pattern is at the moment! In any transaction it is important that the price paid should be one satisfactory to buyer and seller alike, otherwise their on-going relationship will be jeopardised, either by the former feeling cheated or the latter disgruntled by excessive haggling.

Though all the above needs to be taken into account, experience indicates that general guidelines exist for a core of Clarice Cliff items, assuming them to be in good condition, free from restoration and bearing appropriate backstamps. As pattern is paramount, the following guide divides items according to pattern.

Price range 1 covers patterns made in considerable quantity and therefore fairly readily available, including **Crocus**, **Ravel**, **Rhodanthe** and similar.

Price range 2 covers patterns harder to find, being made over a shorter time-span either because of their complexity or through lack of popularity at the time.

Price range 3 covers rare patterns, including experimental ware, and must be regarded as particularly flexible since it is especially subject to current trends. It includes all the paterns made in ranges like **Appliqué**, **Latona** and **Inspiration**, plus special geometric patterns like **Blue W**, **Sliced Circle** and **Lightning**, rare landscapes like **Etna**, **Limberlost** and **Solitude**, and items from Dame Laura Knight and Eva Crofts. Impossible to evaluate except on an individual basis, prices given here are based in the main on known sales.

Note: Not all items, of course, were made in every pattern, and it is not suggested that they were. But surprises are always possible!

Item	Price Range 1
Teaware	
Teacup/saucer, open handle	£75-£95/$130-$165
Teacup/saucer, solid handle	£95-£115/$165-$200
Trio (cup, saucer, plate) open handle	£110-£135/$190-$235
Trio, solid handle	£140-£175/$245-$305
Coffee cup/saucer,open handle	£75-£100/$130-$175
Coffee cup/saucer, solid handle	£85-£120/$150-$210
Plate 23cm	£85-£135/£150-$235
Plate 17.5cm	£50-£80/$85-$140
Sandwich tray, 29.5cm long	£125-£150/$220-$260
Sandwich set (tray + 6 plates)	£425-£550/$745-$965
Biarritz plate 22.5cm wide	£85-£115/$150-$200
Teapot (a) Windsor, Globe, Lynton, Daffodil, Athens	£225-£300/$395-$525
Teapot (b) Bonjour, Conical, Stamford	£300-£400/$525-$700
Teapot (a) with matching milk jug, sugar basin (sometimes also called a "Trio")	£400-£500/$700-$875
Teapot (b) with matching milk jug, sugar basin	£450-£550/$785-$965
Early Morning Set (or Tea for Two) – Teapot, milk jug, sugar basin, 2 cups/saucers, biscuit plate, shapes (b)	£650-£750/$1140-$1315
Coffee Pot shapes (a)	£165-£195/$290-$340
Coffee Pot shapes (b)	£225-£300/$395-$525
Coffee Set shapes (a) for 6	£450-£550/$790-$960
Coffee Set shapes (b) for 6	£650-£850/$1140-$1490
Sugar Basin (round)	£75-£95/$130-$165
Sugar Basin Bonjour, Conical, large	£150-£200/$260-$350
Sugar Basin Bonjour, Conical, small	£125-£150/$220-$260
Teaset 21 piece Shapes (a)	£450-£550/$790-$965
Teaset 21 piece Shapes (b)	£500-£650/$875-$1140
Teaset 23 piece (inc Teapot) Shapes (a)	£700-£800/$1225-$1400

Price Range 2   Price Range 3

Price Range 2	Price Range 3
£125-£150/$220-$260	£250-£650/$435-$1140
£140-£170/$245-$300	£300-£800/$525-$1400
£175-£195/$305-$340	£400-£950/$700-$1662
£195-£225$340-$395	£450-£1200/$790-$2000
£120-£150/$210-$260	£250-£750/$440-$1315
£135-£175/$235-$305	£300-£850/$525-$1490
£135-£185$235-$325	£300-£850+/$525-$1490
£100-£150/$175-$260	£300-£750+/$525-$1315
£150-£185/$260-$325	£400-£800+/$700-$1400
£650-£850/$1140-$1490	£850-£1500/$550-$2625
£135-£165/$235-$290	£400-£1000+/$700-$1760
£300-£450/$525-$790	£600-£1200/$1050-$2100
£400-£550/$700-$965	£750-£1500/$1315-$2625
£450-£550/$785-$965	£900-£1800/$1575-$3150
£550-£650/$965-$1135	£1200-£2000/$1050-$3500
£700-£800/$1225-$1400	£2000-£2750+/$3500-$4815
£200-£250/$350-$435	£500-£750/$875-$1315
£300-£350/$525-$615	£600-£850/$1050-$1490
£600-£750/$1050-$1315	£1500-£2000+/$2625-$3500
£800-£950/$1400-$1660	£2000-£4000+/$3500-$7000
£100-£135/$175-$235	£150-£450/$260-$790
£200-£250/$350-$440	£300-£550/$525-$965
£145-£195/$255-$340	£250-£450/$435-$790
£750-£950/$1315-$1660	£2500-£4500/$4375-$7875
£850-£1000/$1490-$1750	£4000-£6000+/$7000-$10500
£850-£1000/$1490-$1750	£4500-£6500+/$7875-$11375

Item	Price Range 1
Jugs	
Athens, large	£140-£190/$245-$330
Athens, medium	£125-£140/$215-$245
Windsor, Perth, large	£125-£160/$215-$280
Windsor, Perth, medium	£115-£150/$200-$260
Bonjour, Conical, large	£160-£200/$280-$350
Bonjour, Conical, medium	£120-£150/$210-$260
Bonjour, Conical, small	£95-£115/$165-$200
Small, open handle jug	£75-£95/$130-$170
Preserve Pots (with cover)	
Cylindrical preserve pot	£150-£200/$260-$350
Bonjour preserve pot	£200-£250/$350-$440
Beehive honeypot, large	£235-265/$410-$465
Beehive honeypot, small	£200-£235/$350-$415
Apple honeypot, large	£235-£265/$410-$465
Apple honeypot, small	£200-£225/$350-$395
Daffodil preserve pot	£235-£265/$410-$465
Cherry honeypot	£200-£225/$350-$395
Sugar Shakers	
Conical	£200-£250/$350-$440
Bonjour	£200-£250/$350-$440
EPNS topped shaker	£175-£235/$305-$410
Miscellaneous	
Toastrack, large	£175-£225/$305-$395
Toastrack, small	£150-£200/$260-$350
Fruit set (1 large bowl, 6 small)	£400-£600/$660-$1050
Individual fruit bowl	£65-£85/$115-£150
Individual grapefruit dish, flange ends	£95-£135/$165-$235
Cruet (or muffineer) (salt, pepper, mustard pot/cover) Conical, Bonjour	£200-£250/$350-$435

Price Range 2	Price Range 3
£200-£250/$350-$44	£800-£1500/$1400-$2625
£175-£190/$305-$340	£550-£950/$960-$1665
£175-£190/$305-$340	£550-£950/$960-$1665
£135-£150/$235-$265	£400-£850/$700-$1490
£225-£275/$390-$480	£600-£950/$1050-$1665
£200-£235/$350-$410	£500-£850/$875-$1490
£125-£150/$215-$265	£350-£750/$610-$1315
£100-£125/$175-$220	£300-£600/$525-$1050
£200-£250/$350-$440	£500-£750/$875-$1315
£250-£275/$435-$480	£600-£800/$1050-$1400
£275-£300/$480-$525	£650-£950/$1135-$1665
£250-£275/$435-$480	£600-£900/$1050-$1575
£275-£300/$480-$525	£650-£950/$1135-$1665
£250-£275/$435-$480	£600-£900/$1050-$1575
£275-£300/$480-$525	£650-£950/$1135-$1665
£225-£250/$390-$440	£450-£750/$785-$1315
£350-£450/$610-$790	£750-£1000+/1315-$1750
£250-£350/$435-$615	£600-£900/$1050-$1575
£225-£275/$390-$480	£500-£850/$875-$1490
£225-£250/$393-$437	£500-£750/$875-$1315
£200-£250/$350-$437	£400-£600/$700-$1050
£600-£800/$1060-$1400	£1500-£2000/$2625-$3000
£85-£110/$148-$192	£200-£400/$350-$700
£120-£145/$210-$255	£250-£450/$435-$590
£275-£350/$480-$615	£500-£800/$875-$1400

Item	Price Range 1
Cruet, waisted items	£150-£225/$260-$395
Pair salt/pepper, Bonjour, Conical	£150-£200/$260-$350
Pair salt/pepper, waisted	£100-£135/$175-$235
Candlestick, tall, ziggurat	£200-£250/$350-$435
Candlesticks, pair, squat, cube, conical	£250-£300/$435-$525

Patterned Novelties

Item	Price Range 1
Ashtray, coaster	£75-£95/$130-$165
Smoker's set (complete) (tray, 4 ashtrays, cigarette box/cover, matchholder)	£300-£350/$525-$615
Cigarette holder, match holder	£150-£225/$260-$395
Inkwell, complete with covers	£300-£350/$525-$615
Cauldron, large	£150-£225/$260-$395
Cauldron, small	£125-£200/$215-$350
Sabot (or clog), large	£150-£200/$260-$350
Sabot, small	£125-£175/$215-$305
Beakers	£85-£135/$150-$235
Duck eggcup, 6 eggcups	£300-£400/$525-$700
Eggcup set on plate, 4 eggcups	£150-£200/$260-$350
Single eggcup, footed	£55-£65/$95-$115
Single eggcup, squat	£45-£55/$75-$95
Cigarette box/cover	£200-£225/$350-$395
Sardine box, butter box/cover	£225-£250/$390-$440
Muffin dish/cover	£250-£275/$435-$481
Cheese dish/cover	£300-£350/$525-$615
Bookend, single, Teddy Bear, Golliwog, patterned base	£500-£600/$875-$1050
Biscuit barrel/cover shapes 335, 336, cylindrical, EPNS mounted	£200-£250/$435-$790

Vases

Item	Price Range 1
Vase, simple shape, large	£275-£350/$480-$615
Vase, simple shape, small	£225-£300/$390-$525

Price Range 2	Price Range 3
£200-£230/$350-$405	£400-£600/$700-$1050
£200-£230/$350-$405	£300-£500/$525-$875
£140-£175/$245-$305	£250-£400/$435-$700
£275-£300/$480-$525	£450-£750/$785-$1315
£300-£400/$525-$700	£600-£800/$1050-$1400
£100-£150/$175-$265	£200-£700/$350-$1225
£400-£500/$700-$875	£600-£1000+/$1050-$1750
£250-£275/$435-$480	£400-£800/$700-$1400
£350-£500/$610-$875	£600-£1000/$1050-$1750
£250-£300/$435-$525	£450-£850/$785-$1490
£200-£250/$350-$440	£350-£750/$610-$1315
£250-£325/$440-$570	£400-£800/$700-$1400
£200-£250/$350-$440	£350-£700/$610-$1225
£150-£200/$260-$350	£300-£750/$525-$1315
£350-£475/$610-$830	£600-£850/$1050-$1487
£200-£250/$350-$440	£450-£750/$875-$1315
£65-£85/$110-$150	£150-£200/$260-$350
£55-£370/$70-$650	£125-£250/$215-$440
£250-£325/$435-$570	£600-£950/$1050-$1665
£275-£350/$480-$615	£650-£1000/$1135-$1750
£275-£325/$480-$570	£500-£950/$875-$1665
£350-£425/$610-$745	£600-£1000/$1050-$1750
£600-£700/$1050/$1225	£750-£1000/$1310-$1750
£300-£400/$527-$700	£500-£800/$865-$1400
£350-£450/$610-$790	£750-£1000/$1310-$1750
£250-£350/$435-$615	£550-£850/$785-$1490

Item	Price Range 1
Vase, complex shape with fins, flanges etc., large	£350-£425/$610-$745
Vase, complex shape, small	£300-£400/$525-$700
Miniature vases	£200-£300/$350-$525
Flower baskets	£250-£300/$435-$525
Bowls	
Bowl, simple shape, large	£225-£275/$390-$480
Bowl, simple shape, medium	£200-£250/$350-$440
Bowl, simple shape, small	£150-£200/$260-$350
Bowl, complex shape, Daffodil, Conical, stepped etc, large	£350-£400/$610-$700
As above, medium	£300-£350/$525-$615
As above, small	£275-£325/$480-$570
Wall plates and Chargers	
Wall plate, 23cm (decorated surface)	£150-£225/260-$395
Plaques, chargers, 30cm diam	£350-£450/$610-$790
As above, 35cm diam	£450-£550/$785-$965
As above, 40cm diam	£500-£600/$875-$1050
Jardinières, Lotus Jugs, Isis Vases	
Jardinière, large	£300-£400/$525-$700
Jardinière, small	£200-£300/$350-$525
Fern pot	£175-£300/$305-$525
Lotus Jug, single-handled	£400-£500/$700-$875
Lotus Jug, doubled-handled	£450-£550/$785-$965
Isis Vase, large	£400-£600/$700-$1050
Isis Vase, small	£300-£400/$605-$700

Price Range 2

£450-£550/$785-$965
£350-£450/$610-$790
£300-£400/$526-$700
£300-£400/$525-$700

£350-£450/$610-$790
£300-£400/$525-$700
£250-£350/$430-$615
£400-£500/$700-$875

£350-£450/$610-$790
£300-£400/$525-$700

£250-£300/$455-$700
£450-£600/$785-$1050
£550-£700/$960-$1225
£600-£750/$1050-$1315

£450-£550/$785-$965
£350-£400/$610-$700
£300-£350/$525-$615
£450-£550/$785-$965
£550-£750/$960-$1315
£500-£700/$875-$1225
£400-£650/$700-$1140

Price Range 3

£1000-£1500/$1750-$2625
£800-£1000/$1400-$1750
£500-£800/$875-$1400
£550-£850/$785-$1490

£750-£850/$1310-$1490
£600-£750/$1050-$1315
£500-£650/$875-$1140
£800-£1200/$1400-$2100

£750-£1000/$1310-$1750
£650-£800/$1135-$1400

£800-£1200+/$1400-$2100
£1000-£3000+/$1750-$5250
£1500-£3500+/$2625-$6125
£4000-£6000+/$7000-$10500

£700-£950/$1225-$1665
£600-£850/$1050-$1490
£450-£750/$785-$1315
£700-£1000+/$1225-$1750
£950-£3000+/$1660-$5250
£1200-£2500+/$2100-$4375
£800-£2000+/$1400-$3500

Novelties (approximate prices only)

Kneeling figure candleholder (pair)	£200-£250/$350-$440
Bookends – cottages (pair)	£500/875
Bookends – birds, showgirl & student, etc	£550/$965
Toothbrush holders – Teddy Bear, Golliwog	£550/$965
Chick cocoapot, with tray and beaker	£350-£400/$610-$700
Teepee teapot	£350+/$615
Bookends (pair) shape	£405/$710
various patterns	£300+/$525
Viking longboat, various patterns	£300-£400/$525-$700
Flying Swan flowerholder, various patterns	£300/$525
Rock flowerholder, 2 sizes, various patterns	£55-£75/$95-$130
Napkin rings (square)	£100+/$175
Napkin rings, novelty shape, elephant etc	£75-£95/$130-$165
Display plaques 8.5cm long, used by retailers to identify patterns	£300-£600/$525-$1050
Star Signs	£400/$700
Lido Lady ashtray	£300/$525
Wall masks, wall pockets	£200-£300/$350-$525
"Age of Jazz" figures	each £4000-£5000/$7000-$8750
Toby Jugs – Small	£150/$260
Medium	£200/$350
Large	£300/$525
Character	£400-£500/$700-$875

Commissioned Work

Produced by Clarice Cliff from designs by famous artists of her day, these in general fetch slightly less than equivalent Clarice Cliff designs, the exceptions being work by Dame Laura Knight, especially her **Circus** range, prices being between £2500/$4375 and £11000/$19250, and Eva Crofts, the textile designer (**Tea for Two** £2500/$4375).

Later Ranges

Previously less popular ranges, like **My Garden**, **Celtic Harvest**, **Waterlily** and the 1937 design, **Fruit and Basket**, are now becoming increasingly popular, but are not as yet reaching prices like those above. A **Celtic Harvest** teapot usually fetches around £250/$440, the two sizes of jugs £175/$306 and £125/$220, with others under £100/$175, **My Garden** being in the same price range. Apart from the large **Waterlily** planter, £175-£250/$305-$440, most **Waterlily** items are £50-£100/$85-$175, as are those in the **Fruit and Basket** range. Increasing popularity is, of course, likely to cause rises in this area.

Notes for Collectors

Starting a Clarice Cliff Collection

Many Clarice Cliff collections have been started more or less by accident, one or two pieces being inherited and then added to in order to form a small display, which has then grown by gifts and purchases to the point at which it has become an absorbing interest. Other collectors have begun by looking for pottery to display on, say, a dresser or a set of shelves, and having got together a suitable selection have found that buying Clarice Cliff pieces has been so enjoyable they don't want to give it up. It might also be said to be addictive, and when pieces are discovered in good condition and at the right price, they are very hard to resist. Perhaps the pattern with the most perennial appeal is **Autumn Crocus**. Originally the most popular in Clarice Cliff's own day, it still remains the one most frequently chosen by first time purchasers. Only later do they gain confidence to add to their collection the more outrageous colour combinations of **Sunray**, **Gardenia** or **Umbrellas & Rain**, **Spring Crocus** is a gentle feminine pattern which is easy to live with; **Melon** is a striking addition to a sophisticated interior and **Celtic Harvest** is the exact opposite, looking its best in a cottage style interior. So wide is the range of Clarice Cliff's work that there is something which will appeal to everybody. The only problem lies in deciding what and how to collect. Most people begin by collecting indiscriminately and only later decide to set parameters for themselves, selling off early purchases which no longer fit in with now established tastes and preferences.

A display limited to one favourite pattern can be very impressive, since all resources have been devoted to a single objective: to get together as many different pieces as possible of the chosen pattern. The opposite extreme is to aim to cover as many patterns as possible. Since Clarice Cliff is estimated to have designed around 2000 patterns altogether it is unlikely that anyone will manage to find them all! This is an approach which is attractive, as it allows a quick start to a collection, limited only by the financial budget of the purchaser.

A third way might well be to emulate the original purchasers of Clarice Cliff pottery by buying items selected to fit in with your existing decor. This is a sensible approach, since whichever method you choose you will always be limited by the available space, and by this system you will be buying particular pieces for particular places in your home.

Another approach is to select a shape which fits you pocket and your surroundings. Where plenty of money and plenty of wall space are available, a display of plates is perhaps the most decorative way of showing off a range of patterns, combined with plaques and chargers.

It is worth noting that chargers are dish shaped and the plaques plate shaped, though they were made in the same sizes and both were usually wall hung. Chargers, though, could be used as fruit dishes or even paired together in a wooden frame to make a two-tier 'occasional' table. A display of plaques and chargers alone would be stunning but may also be prohibitively expensive. If space is limited, as well as finance, a collection of smaller items would be effective; coffee cans perhaps or 'trios' (cup, saucer and tea plate) for instance.

One shape which displays particularly well is the *Conical* sugar shaker, since this allows patterns to be seen very effectively and a variation might be to include *Conical* salt and pepper shakers too, contrasting the large with the small. A miniature collection would be ideal for a single cabinet including perhaps ash trays, coasters, cauldrons, toast racks and the smaller candlesticks. The ultimate, of course, would be a collection of *Lotus* jugs and *Isis* vases, but few collectors are likely to contemplate such an outlay.

Record Keeping

If your collection has been begun by an inheritance or by pieces given to you by elderly relatives, you may find as your collection grows that you want to exchange some of your original items for more suitable additions. Damaged items, too, bought perhaps for the sake of acquiring a rare pattern or unusual shape, will probably be replaced once perfect specimens become available. You may be in a position to buy frequently, or your budget may limit you to the occasional purchase. Gifts may come your way at certain times of the year and if these are out of line with your existing pieces it is useful to know a friendly dealer who will take them in part exchange for something else, or possibly sell them for you on a sale or return basis. But however you get your collection together and whatever your guiding principle, it is essential to keep a written record of your transactions, perhaps with photographs as well, giving each purchase a number and writing down its cost, the date purchased, who sold it to you and a brief description of its shape, pattern and condition. This is vitally important because if and when you decide to sell it, you will need to think back perhaps several years – not something easily done from memory. Though the main pleasure of collecting is the beauty of the pieces individually and together, the bonus that it will probably be a good investment cannot be overlooked, and even if you never sell a single piece of it your record is proof that you have spent your money wisely as prices rise – and there is every indication that they will continue to do so.

Insurance

This talk of monetary values raises the question of insurance. A modest collection can usually be included in your general household insurance but it is essential to raise the matter with your insurers in case there is a top limit and you have acquired one or more very expensive items – a *Lotus* jug for example. Also, one must be aware of parts and sets because if you have a tea or coffee set and you break one cup, that one cup may be all you will be covered for, even though a set worth several hundred pounds has been ruined. Larger collections will require a separate insurance and should be updated each year to take into account new purchases and rising prices, and equally any selling off which may have taken place.

The premium is naturally proportionate to the total value of the collection but the peace of mind will be worth it. One way to bring it down a little is to install a burglar alarm and special locks on at least the windows and doors of the room where the collection is kept. However, average collectors should be careful not to let these precautions spoil their pleasure in having the collection. It seems very unlikely that anyone would deliberately set out to steal fragile objects like pottery, when more portable items like jewellery and silver provide less hazardous targets, so the main danger your collection is in will be accidental damage rather than theft. If an item does get broken, or even just cracked or chipped, you will need to decide how to approach the insurance company. Polaroid photographs of the broken pieces are invaluable, especially if accompanied by a signed letter from a reputable dealer to the effect that such and such an item, current market value £x, has been seen "damaged beyond repair" or "damaged but restorable at a cost of £x". It is important to note that restoration will reduce the value of the item by quite a proportion. Depending on its extent, this reduction should be stated and claimed for in your application.

Restoration

Restoration is, in fact, a question fraught with "ifs and buts". There is all the difference in the world between knowingly buying a restored piece and buying one by accident, only finding the restoration afterwards. If restoration is pointed out by the seller, and you decide to buy the piece nevertheless (perhaps because it is a rare pattern which you are unlikely to find elsewhere), this is quite acceptable and the price will take the restoration into account. One caution though: be careful to note in your collection record not only that the piece is restored but where the restoration has been carried out. New techniques and modern materials are constantly coming into use, making restoration very difficult to detect, so trust is essential between buyer and seller. If you buy a piece on which you later find restoration, the item should be taken back to the seller – who should refund your money – "Caveat emptor", or "let the buyer beware" is not a motto by which a dealer can trade if he values his reputation and wants to build up a circle of regular and satisfied customers. It is always wise to examine any item very thoroughly in a good light. Spouts and handles should be checked with particular care and a finger run round rims and bases, as touch is often a better guide than sight. Look out, too, for any slight variation in colour. The chemical composition of the colours used in Clarice Cliff's day are in some cases now no longer permitted for reasons of health and safety and modern colours are usually fairly easy to detect when in close proximity to the original handpainting.

Lighting and Display

As your collection grows you will eventually find that the original space allotted to it becomes too small. What then? One appropriate solution, if you can find room for it, is an Art Deco china cabinet, a simple, angular one if you prefer, or perhaps an eye-catching circular one if the rest of your decor can accommodate it. After all, a large proportion of Clarice Cliff's output was probably displayed in just such cabinets throughout the Thirties, though you will perhaps want to add a modern touch by introducing some unobtrusive lighting to show off your pieces, the glass shelves letting the light shine through from top to bottom. If you feel something more up-to-date will fit your room better, adjustable glass shelves housed in an alcove can be fitted, with sliding glass doors to keep out dust, again with suitable lighting. Aluminium and glass cases of the kind found in jewellery or antiques shops are also widely available but these may seem to you too much like turning your home into a museum, though they are excellent for office displays or foyers. As a background to your collection, however you display it, framed posters from the various Clarice Cliff exhibitions are ideal, or perhaps reproductions of original Bizarre advertisements.

Rarity

Despite the Depression, and thanks to designers like Clarice Cliff, the Thirties were years of high output in the pottery industry and competition was keen among the leading manufacturers like Wilkinsons, Fieldings, Shelley and Myott. Had all the pottery that was produced survived, there would have been ample for all of today's collectors, but in fact much of the output was tableware, used constantly and frequently broken. Decorative objects like vases and flower jugs were in less danger, but they too occasionally came to grief in the course of accidental encounters with household pets or an over zealous cleaner. The Second World War led to the putting away of superfluous items of decoration "for the duration" and boxes of pottery and ornaments were stored more or less safely in the loft along with pictures whose glass, shattered in an air raid, might cause injury. Sometimes the boxes were brought down again after the war, sometimes not. Changing tastes condemned their contents as 'old fashioned' and much Thirties pottery was thrown out or given to jumble sales where it was sold for a few pence. What had been a flood of brightly coloured, handpainted pottery before the war was reduced to a trickle. In consequence, the rediscovery of Clarice Cliff and the rising demand for her work throughout the Seventies and Eighties found only a comparatively small amount available in the market place. If this was true of the once ubiquitous **Autumn Crocus**, it was even more true of patterns originally produced for only a limited period. In other words, all Clarice Cliff is rare, but some patterns are rarer than others and some shapes are very rare indeed.

Perhaps the rarest range of all is **Inspiration** and as in Clarice's own day, it is always expensive. Similarly, so are the ranges in other experimental techniques like **Latona** and **Applique**. Early geometric Bizarre Ware is also very rare and very prized by serious collectors. Variations on the **Crocus** theme, the **Blue Crocus** and the rarer **Purple Crocus** are very sought after, while **Sunray** and **House & Bridge** are two patterns which always fetch high prices. *Tennis* is another rare pattern and *Butterfly* too is seldom seen for sale, while **Cowslip** (in green and particularly in blue) is exceptionally rare. Of the later patterns, **Forest Glen** is one of the most unusual and difficult to find. Items from the pottery designed by famous artists of the day are novelties which enhance any collection, especially those of Dame Laura Knight's Circus range. These are always worth watching out for as they add interest by providing a variation to the main collection which was designed by Clarice herself. It is easy to see which shapes are likely to be the rare ones, as any unusual fins or flanges meant a risk of warping in the kiln, while pieces obviously made in several sections joined together were expensive to produce and were only made in small quantities, to be further reduced by their fragility and consequent breakages.

As time passes, various factors operate to affect the collecting fields. Books, articles, television programmes and much publicised auctions act as catalysts. On the one hand they arouse interest and make more people keen to buy Clarice Cliff pieces and on the other they bring out of hiding fresh examples of her work from people who did not previously realise they were sitting on a gold mine. Also, more people are now dealing in Art Deco in general, many of them with a bias towards the Pottery Ladies and this means there is a wider spread of specialist shops and stalls in antique markets, as well as Art Deco fairs in London and elsewhere. However the proven investment value of Clarice Cliff means that as important pieces disappear into private collections, they are unlikely to reappear on the open market again. Thus, although from time to time prices may stabilise there is only a limited amount to satisfy demand and any stimulus from the media can send prices rocketing up again.

Availability and Sources

Supposing, then you have decided to start buying Clarice Cliff or to add to the pieces you already own? You will have to be prepared to put in much time and effort as well as money if you are to achieve more than merely average success. Apart from the specialist auctions of Clarice Cliff pottery, held mainly in London, and the occasional pieces in general auctions across the country, probably the best way to add to your collection is to get to know the specialist Art Deco dealers in your own area and then range further afield, making your wants known. A phone call first is advisable as closing days vary from town to town and there is nothing worse than travelling a long distance only to find the shop you plan to visit is closed. An advantage with this plan is that established dealers have their reputations to consider and are likely to be keen to build up a client list with a view to future sales, so transactions with them will be smooth and satisfactory. Buying at a shop or in an antiques centre is a more leisurely affair than at auction, and you can probably obtain reassuring information as to provenance in many cases, which adds to the interest of the piece and sometimes helps in dating. Prices, too, are usually fixed with an eye to future sales to regular customers, though overheads and therefore profit margins inevitably vary in different parts of the country. At auction there's always the chance of a bargain but equally the danger of paying too much in the heat of the moment, as well as the buyer's premium to consider. Probably both carefully considered purchases over a shop counter and successful bids at auction must go into the building up of a serious collection.

Then, of course, there are the fairs. Nowadays most fairs include dealers selling Art Deco pottery and on their stalls there are sometimes pieces by Clarice Cliff, as well as some that crop up on the more general stalls. People often have the impression that public admission times mean that most of the important dealing is done within the trade before the public are allowed to enter, but provided you get to a fair early it is possible to find choice pieces which have only just been unwrapped and put out to fill up spaces. Many fairs now have early admission at a higher price, which you may find it worthwhile to pay as it puts you on a footing with visiting trade buyers. Some fairs, too, are now so huge that the earlier you start your visit the better, especially as often there are hundreds of outside pitches as well as those under cover in the main pavilions. Of more specific interest are the specialist Art Deco fairs where there is likely to be some Clarice Cliff pottery on nearly every stall, unless the dealer is selling, say mainly lighting or furniture. Twenty years ago Art Deco fairs were few and far between, and collectors looked forward to them for months ahead. Now they have increased in number till there seems to be one almost every week, with occasional clashes when two are held on the same day. While this proliferation reflects the increasingly popularity of the 1920s and 1930s, it has also spread more thinly the available stock for dealers and collectors alike, especially as many of the choicest pieces are reserved for the big London auctions or prestige events like the antiques fairs at the National Exhibition Centre. For this reason alone it is important to foster good relations with the dealers you know and trust, so that your collection will benefit from the best they have on offer.

While there is little point in asking a dealer to "ring me when you have any Clarice Cliff in", a specific request will often bring results, as a dealer will watch out on his travels for items he knows he can sell as soon as he gets home again by means of a single phone call. Similarly, let other collectors know what lines you are following, so that if they are offered pieces they don't want themselves they will bear you in mind. If they have pieces you covet, drop a hint or two, so that if they decide to sell they will give you a 'first refusal'. Keep an eye on auctioneers' advertisements as they will usually mention any Clarice Cliff items they have on offer in the small print and while the big auction houses attract dealers from all over the country, smaller firms in your own area may go unnoticed except by the local trade, which may not include anyone bidding on 'modern' pottery. Getting to know a porter who will bid for you saves hours of tedious sitting in auction rooms and is well worth the occasional tip to keep him happy.

Most dealers, thanks to the Pottery Ladies series and headline auctions, are au fait with Clarice Cliff prices and may indeed be highly over-optimistic regarding their prices for quite ordinary pieces that come their way, but there is always the chance that a small gem may turn up in your local junk shop or perhaps at a school bazaar where the organisers have failed to have their bric-a-brac checked by a local dealer. If you do make a discovery, it is as well to be generous, especially if the function is for charity. Paying a little more than you are asked, provided the item is worth it, will ensure that on another occasion you are offered any similar items, perhaps being given 'first pick'. So be sure to leave your phone number. If a **Crocus** jampot was sent to the jumble sale this time, next time the sender may decide to get rid of their **Sunray Lotus** jug – who knows?

Information about fairs, shops and auctions can be found in a number of ways. Those in your own area will usually be advertised in your local press, while magazines for collectors carry advertisements for those further afield. For a really comprehensive coverage it is possible to subscribe to the trade press, that is, the *Antiques Trade Gazette* and the *Antiques Bulletin*, both weekly and available on subscription, but also sold at many major fairs. Useful, too, is the smaller monthly publication *The Collector*, and the annual *Guide to the Antique Shops of Great Britain* is handy to keep in the car. Fairs guides are proliferating, too, as for more and more people collecting antiques of all kinds is becoming an absorbing hobby, and these can be bought at fairs, while most organisers put out free leaflets with information about the dates and venues of their future events.

Armed with information from some or all of these sources, it will be possible to plan your time to the best advantage, and your collection will benefit from you being in the right place at the right time, that combination of hard work and good luck which lies behind the building up of every successful collection.

In the Clarice Style — Reproductions and Derivations

As interest in Clarice Cliff pottery increased, alongside it grew up a whole world of "spin-off" items, ranging from knitwear to greetings cards, produced in the Clarice style. All paid homage, more or less successfully, to her vivid colours and instantly recognisable patterns, adapted to suit different shapes and textures in a way compared to the specially-embroidered table napkins and tray cloths produced in her own day to go with her tableware. Hand-knitted sweaters began to be seen at Art Deco fairs with bold adaptation of Clarice Cliff landscapes, and not long afterwards the patterns became available in book form – *Art Deco Knits* by Melinda Coss. Brooches were made from shards of original Clarice Cliff pottery, the edges smoothly polished and a pin attached to the back, while tiny Stamford teapots, also brooches, were soon on sale. Watercolours of flowers in her vases and of her Tea for Two sets were reproduced as cards for collectors to send to each other, and members of the flourishing Clarice Cliff Collectors Club could buy specially-produced enamel badges with a different pattern annually. But this was only the beginning . . .

One of Clarice Cliff's own paintresses, Marjory Higginson, who had worked for Clarice Cliff from 1928 to 1941 and from 1952 to 1958, began to produce her own range of Clarice's patterns, not copying them exactly, owing to the use of modern materials and a china body, but skilfully decorated and very reminiscent of the items of the early Bizarre days. These were offered for sale through the Clarice Cliff Collectors Club and proved quite popular, as prices were reasonable and as tableware they were not to expensive to use. At the other end of the scale, Clarice Cliff related limited edition items were soon being produced in the Potteries on behalf of a London-based commercial firm, Kevin Francis Ceramics, starting with a Clarice Cliff toby jug, eventually made in several sizes, in a successful range later expanded to include other famous figures from the world of ceramics. Figurines of Clarice Cliff are also available, and so is a profile wall-mask which really does capture much of her charm. All these items were bought by Clarice Cliff collectors and by collectors of limited edition pottery alike, and their success encouraged the firm to go on to produce many more items in the Art Deco style.

A short-lived but interesting experiment was the production by the famous firm of Osborne and Little of a wallpaper decorated with pieces of Clarice Cliff pottery, but perhaps to live with every day this was just too vivid and too eye-catching, and it is no longer available. However, more recently another famous firm, Liberty, used a **Capri** *Bonjour* teapot and milk jug to illustrate one of their magazine advertisements for a range of furnishing fabrics, the text reading "The early 1930s Art Deco pottery of Clarice Cliff . . . has inspired one part of the collection". The firm of Past Times, too, who sell "Decorative accessories and gifts inspired by the past", have a "Blue Flrs" cardigan, a lamp-base decorated with a Coral Firs-type pattern of trees and a pair of angular bone china mugs with brightly-coloured landscapes similar in style though not in colour to those of Clarice Cliff.

Bone china has also been used for a series of limited edition plates produced by Wedgwood known as the "Bizarre and Clarice Cliff Collection of Living Landscapes", in which the colours are very close to the originals. Issued as a series of 12 through the Bradford Exchange and selling at just under £20 each, these plates are intended for sale purely on decorative appeal, while Wedgwood's other Clarice Cliff reproductions are aimed more specifically at collectors of her work. Developed by the Mason's Ironstone division of Wedgwoods, with the benefit of advice from the Chairman of the Clarice Cliff Collectors Club, it was intended that the reproductions – clearly marked as such! – would allow collectors to add to their collections at moderate prices a rare shape or pattern otherwise out of their price-range. Initial response was sufficiently good to encourage Wedgwood to add further shapes and patterns, so probably this has proved to be one of the more successful attempts to follow in Clarice's footsteps.

Interestingly, an earlier set of reproductions, produced by Midwinter in 1985, appears to have sold less well. Midwinter took over the factory shortly after Colley Shorter's death, at the point when Clarice Cliff herself retired, and the reproductions included a *Mei Ping* vase in **Honolulu**, a 33cm charger in **Summerhouse**, an **Umbrellas and Rain** *Conical* sugarbowl and *Conical* sugar shakers in six patterns. These items were also clearly marked as reproduction, and there was no intention to deceive. Prices ranged from just under £30 for a shaker to almost £300 for the vase. Despite disappointing sales – some of the shakers were once seen reduced to half-price in a sale! – for one collector at least they proved a good investment. At the Christie's Clarice Cliff auction in November, 1992, a complete set of them fetched nearly £2000.

Production problems included the fact that some of the colours used by the Bizarre Girls are now banned, since they contain toxic substances like cadmium and lead, and substitutes had to be found. Also, the staff in the Midwinter decorating department needed retraining in the style of freehand painting current in Clarice Cliff's own day in order to achieve the authentic freedom of execution and the correct weight of colour. Ten of the original paintresses were still alive and were called in to advise on quality control and painting techniques.

Not everyone in the world of Clarice Cliff collectors wholeheartedly approved of the project, some finding it gimmicky and an attempt to cash in on Clarice's growing popularity, but in many ways it was a compliment to the timeless quality of her designs. The Midwinter experiment was reported in enthusiastic terms in the media, most of the articles giving a resume of Clarice Cliff's life, which stressed the 'avant garde' nature of her work and, rather touchingly, reported that a Midwinter paintress, Pat Walters, could be seen at Harrods' Wedgwood Room demonstrating the hand painting of Clarice Cliff patterns, just as the Bizarre Girls did in their berets and floppy bow ties, 40 years before. Nor was Clarice's all time best seller forgotten – a modern adaptation was made of **Crocus** for reproduction on Midwinter's Stonehenge teaware.

No doubt there will be many more items of all kinds to come which owe their inspiration directly or indirectly to Clarice Cliff. Some will be quite acceptable for what they are, while others will stray so far from her original style as to set the purists understandably shuddering. But whatever lies ahead, no doubt Clarice Cliff herself would have been quite happy about it. After all, as they used to say in her own day, "Imitation is the sincerest form of flattery".

Fakes

Early in 1986, Clarice Cliff collectors were alarmed to read in the press that fake *Lotus* vases had begun to turn up in London and before long, elsewhere. Investigation proved, however, that the fakes were so poorly produced that they could be spotted fairly easily and all the major London auction houses refused to handle suspect vases offered to them once the initial alert had gone out. Though considerable trouble had been taken to reproduce exactly the Bizarre backstamp, patchy, uneven toffee-coloured Honeyglaze was a giveaway, while the unglazed bottom rim was narrow compared with the genuine vase. Not only this but the standard of painting was so poor that neither Clarice Cliff nor the art director of any reputable pottery would have accepted it. The inefficiency of the producers of the bogus vases was irritating, to say the least. After all, they were peddling large pieces and hoping for high prices – anyone likely to be paying such large sums of money would have sufficient knowledge to suspect anything so obviously substandard.

Phillips, the auctioneers, with commendable speed, issued an identikit, consisting of three coloured photographs, showing a genuine **Summerhouse** *Lotus* vase and a fake geometric vase. These pictures are top, bottom and sideways on, accompanied by a list of points to watch out for when offered a doubtful piece.

For dealers and collectors the scare was short lived but for the general public the effect lasted longer and occasionally, even today, those fakes are nervously mentioned by people who have seen only the sensational headlines and not read the real facts of the matter.

Unfortunately, it seems possible that the question of fakes will once again be in the news, as recently badly-faked *Conical* sugar shakers and at least two Lotus jugs have surfaced in the Midlands, but have been swiftly detected owing to the poor quality of the painting and also the low price – £80 for something which, if genuine, would cost three times as much. Trading Standards officers have been alerted and once again the problem is being speedily resolved, so perhaps this time shock-horror headlines will be avoided.

Far more serious is the rumour that arises from time to time that a different form of faking is in operation – that of adding Clarice Cliff patterns, usually the more sought after ones like **House & Bridge** to plain items already genuinely backstamped "Clarice Cliff". Advice is sometimes given, "When in doubt, coin it!" That is, scratch the suspect paintwork with the edge of a coin or something similar. Few collectors, however, are likely to have the nerve to risk damaging a valuable item – to say nothing of enraging an honest dealer! – by dragging a coin across the paintwork of a plate or jug. Everyone knows that the surface of perfectly genuine pieces may have been scratched in the course of normal wear, even though the on-glaze handpainting was given a final firing to protect it, and also that some colours, especially dark blue, were fugitive and faded with use.

Again, modern detergents can sometimes have a disastrous effect, as for instance, when the oranges on Crown Ducal **Orange Tree** turn brown with the use of washing up liquid containing bleach. A collector's best protection is to buy from a reputable dealer with, if possible, some indication of the item's provenance. However, the safest rule, guaranteed to avoid altercations, acrimony and regrets is, "When in doubt, don't buy it".

Newly Popular Patterns

In the early days of what we might call the Clarice Cliff Revival, in the main collectors were keen to buy the brightly-coloured early **Bizarre** and **Fantasque** ranges, with Inspiration being favoured by wealthy collectors and post-Bizarre patterns being less favoured on the whole. Certainly ranges like **Celtic Harvest**, **My Garden** and **Waterlily**, along with the newly-identified **Fruit and Basket** range of 1937, were not avidly collected and could be bought very reasonably indeed. Recently this has begun to change, as collectors came to realise how effective each of these patterns could look displayed as a collection, and now prices are rising in response to increased demand.

Celtic Harvest, a chunky range glazed in warm cream with embossed corn motifs and with coloured fruit and poppies on the handles and knobs, occasionally had chrome rims or lids. Teapots appear quite often, as do ewers in two sizes and jampots, either shallow ones or globe-shaped with small feet. Biscuit barrels, fruit bowls and cake dishes are also fairly common, but the attractive sauce-boat with the handle shaped like a scythe, is difficult to find, especially with its accompanying saucer, while teacups, saucers and plates are almost impossible to find, and a collector of this pattern would probably pay very highly for them.

My Garden is a vast range of jugs and vases in various sizes from very large to very small, with a few useful items also appearing, like sugar sifters and candleholders. Usually with flowers embossed heavily on the lower half or on the handle, many of these items are in matt-glazed mushroom, while others have a shiny drip-glaze in brown and yellow called **Sunrise**, a pretty green called **Verdant**, a dramatic silky black, or, perhaps the most attractive of all, **Flame Red**. The fact that this range was made in such a wide range of shapes and colourways indicates that in its own day it was popular, and the signs are that its popularity is on the increase once again.

In the **Waterlily** range, the most familiar item is the largest, the oval waterlily-shaped planter sometimes called the lilypad. It was made in two sizes, usually in pink or yellow, though the fact that one has been seen in green may indicate it could be made to special order, perhaps to match soft furnishings. This shape is also seen in cream with touches of pink and a brownish green, when it matches the cream colourway of the rest of the range, the alternate main colour being a pale blue. As well as the large planter, the range also came in many other shapes and a teapot, biscuit barrel, cheese-dish and salad-bowl with servers were all made. A butter-plate, honeypot, cream jug, milk jug and sugar basin were also available, with two oval dishes and two round ones completing the range. Pretty rather than sophisticated, it nevertheless has a charm of its own, and in either of the two main colourways it displays well on shelves or a dresser in a kitchen.

Finally, only recently identified as being originally called **Fruit and Basket** and dating from 1937, is a range of ware decorated with a basket weave effect and embossed with moulded colourful fruit in purple, pink and green. This range appears to have rarely carried the current Clarice Cliff backstamp, though it is sometimes seen, and so far collectors have discovered a lemonade set of a jug and six beakers with handles, a cylindrical jampot, a large fruit bowl, a biscuit barrel with a cane handle, a sauce boat and saucer, a cheese dish and a cress dish. Probably there are other pieces to come. At present still very reasonably priced – from £25 to £75 – again this is a quieter but attractive pattern which can be very decorative displayed together.

Clarice Cliff Chronology

1899   Clarice Cliff born January 20, at 19 Meir Street, Tunstall, Staffordshire. The family later moved to Edwards Street, Tunstall.
Father:- Harry Thomas Cliff, an iron moulder. Mother:- Ann Cliff, née Machin. Brothers:- Harry, Frank. Sisters:- Sarah, Hannah, Dorothy, Ethel, Nellie.

1909   Left the High Street Elementary School to go to the Summerbank Road School.

1912   Left school to learn freehand painting at Lingard, Webster & Co., Swan Pottery, Tunstall.

1915   Left the Swan Pottery to learn lithography at Hollinshead & Kirkham, Unicorn Pottery, Tunstall. Attended evening classes at Tunstall School of Art, later transferring to Burslem School of Art.

1916   Joined A.J. Wilkinson's Royal Staffordshire Pottery, Burslem.

1920   Wilkinson's took over the Newport Pottery in Newport Lane, Burslem, adjoining their site. Clarice Cliff promoted to work as a gilder, with John Butler and Fred Ridgeway, Wilkinson's leading designers, on the Tibetan, Oriflamme and Rubaiyat ranges.

1923   The Wilkinson Archives has a note 'C.C. does the gold', referring to Pattern No.7309 on a plaque by Fred Ridgeway.

1924   Early figurines, including two men in Arab dress marked 'Clarice C 24' and an old market woman marked 'C.C.24'.

1925   Clarice Cliff moved to 40 Snow Hill, Hanley, a one-bedroom flat over a beauty salon. She was given a studio in Newport pottery with facilities to produce the firm's publicity photographs. Comment was caused by her close association with Colley Shorter, the firm's managing director, a married man 17 years her senior.

1927   Between March 14 and May 26, Clarice Cliff took a short course in sculpture at the Royal College of Art at her employers' expense, her address being given as Campbell House, 90 Sutherland Terrace, Maida Vale, W8. Later this year she visited Paris, again at her employers' expense, to study Continental design. Returning to Newport Pottery, she began decorating a large stock of old-fashioned whiteware with brightly-coloured geometric patterns. A 15-year-old apprentice, Gladys Scarlett, assisted her.

1928   More apprentices – Annie Berisford, Mary Brown, Nellie Harrison, Clara Thomas, Nancy Liversedge, Vera Rawlinson and Cissie Rhodes – joined the team, enabling a production line to be set up. Joan Shorter Baby Ware was launched, based by Clarice Cliff on drawings by Colley Shorter's eight-year-old daughter.
Bizarre, the name chosen by Clarice Cliff, began to be used in July. Soon her name was added. The first press advertisement for **Bizarre Ware** appeared in August backed up by an in-store demonstration in London and a preview at the British Industries Fair.
In September, Ewart Oakes, Wilkinson's chief salesman, took **Bizarre Ware** to

sell in Berkshire. His success led to more orders, and more apprentices, boys as well as girls, were added to the team.

A Bizarre backstamp was created, including Clarice Cliff's signature. Later this year **Crocus** began and continued in various versions until 1963. **Lupin** was also entered into the pattern-book but does not seem to have been put into production.

1929   **Fantasque** introduced as an additional range name.

Shapes: *Archaic* and *Conical*, Patterns included Diamonds, Garland, Lightning, **Lodore**, **Kandina**, **Broth** (until 31) **Inspiration** (31) **Latona** (31) **Latona** tree (30) **Lily** (30) **Ravel** (35) **Sunray** (30) **Trees and House** (31) **Umbrellas and Rain** (30).

By the end of the year, the whole of the Newport Pottery was given over to **Bizarre Ware**.

1930   Shapes: *Stamford* and *Eton* table-ware. **Age of Jazz** figures. Patterns included Branch & Squares, Carpet, **Flora**, **Floreat**, Orange Battle, **Orange House**, **Persian (2)**, Sliced Fruit, Sunburst, Tulip and Leaves, Yoo Hoo. **Applique Avignon** (until 31) **Applique Lucerne** (32) **Applique** Windmill (31) **Autumn** (34) **Berries** (31) **Inspiration Knight Errant** (31) **Latona Dahlia** (31) **Melon** (33) **Oranges** (31) **Original Delecia** (31) **Scraphito** (31).

1931   Shapes: *Stamford* fancies and *Daffodil*. *Conical* sugar dredger

Nuage and **Cafe Au Lait** techniques.

Patterns included: **Tennis**, **Marigold**, **Woodland**, **Applique Idyll** (until 35) Bobbins (33) **Farmhouse** (32) **Gardenia** (32) **Gibraltar** (32) **House & Bridge** (33) **Mountain** (32) **Etna** (32).

1932   Shapes: *Chick* cocoa pot and *Elephant* napkin rings

Patina and **Damask Rose** techniques

Patterns included **Forest Leaves**, **Hollyrose**, **Canterbury Bells** (until 33) **Chintz** (33) **Delecia Citrus** (33) **May Avenue** (33) **Orange Roof Cottage** (33) **Sungay** (33)

Initiation of experiment to involve artists in production of designs for tableware.

1933   commissioned work from artists in production.

Shapes: *Bonjour* and *Biarritz* tableware.

Goldstone range, *Lynton* shapes, Blackbird pie funnels, facemasks **Marlene**, **Flora**, **Chahar**

Patterns included Car And Skyscraper, **Devon**, **Japan**, **Solitude**, **Coral Firs** (until 36) **Cowslip** (34), **Delecia Pansy** (34) **Delecia Poppy** (34) **Honolulu** (34) **Secrets** (37) **Windbells** (34)

1934   Display of commissioned work – 'Modern Art for the table'. **Fantasque** phased out.

Shape: *Trieste*

Patterns included **Bridgewater**, **Newport**, Stencilled Deer, **Hydrangea** (until 35) **Moselle** (or 35) **Rhodanthe** (until 41 and post-war) **Viscaria** (36).

1935	Late in the year, Bizarre phased out. Patterns included **Fragrance**, **Pine Grove**, **Aurea** (until 37) **Cherry Blossom** (36) **Trallee** (36).
1936	Patterns included **Kelverne**, **Passion Fruit**, **Forest Glen** (until 37) Honiton (37) **My Garden** (until 41 and Post-war) **Raffia** (37) **Taormina** (37).
1937	Shapes: *Windsor*, Gnome Nursery Ware. Patterns included **Ferndale**, **Delecia Anemone** (38).
1938	Shapes: **Celtic Harvest** (until 41 and Post-war), Waterlily Range, Signs of the Zodiac.
1939	September, outbreak of war. November 2 death of Mrs Annie Shorter.
1940	December 21, Marriage of Clarice Cliff and And Arthur Colley Austin Shorter (not announced until November 1941).
1941	Newport Pottery requisitioned by the government.
1942	No more decorated pottery for the duration of the war.
1945	Ending of hostilities. Decorated pottery resumed for export only. Restrictions gradually eased.
1952	Wartime restrictions finally lifted completely. Coronation ware produced.
1963	December – Colley Shorter died, aged 81.
1964	Factories sold to Midwinters and Clarice Cliff retired.
1972	Brighton Museum held the first British exhibition of Clarice Cliff pottery, to which she contributed catalogue notes and items from her own collection, some of which she later gave to the Museum. October 23, Clarice Cliff died after a brief illness, aged 73.

Notes

Notes

Francis Joseph
Collector's Register

Join the **Francis Joseph Clarice Cliff Collectors Register**. Registration is free and you will receive a newsletter twice yearly with news of auctions, events, sales and new publications on your particular collecting interest.

Join our register listing your top ten Clarice Cliff designs by filling in the form provided or write to:

*The Francis Joseph Clarice Cliff
Collectors Register,
15 St Swithuns Road, London SE13 6RW
or to
PO Box 69, 4763 Miami FL33269, USA*

MUIR HEWITT

DISCOVER THE WORLD OF ART DECO ORIGINALS
A WIDE SELECTION OF PERIOD CERAMICS BY
CLARICE CLIFF, CHARLOTTE RHEAD, SUSIE COOPER
FURNITURE • MIRRORS • LAMPS • CHROME

Photography by KEITH PAISLEY @ Tel: 01830 520035

J A Z Z

POSTERS AVAILABLE:

AN A2 FULL COLOUR POSTER PRICE £7.50 (+ £2.50 P&P) AND A MATCHING GREETING CARD
PRICED AT £1.95 EACH ARE NOW AVAILABLE. (CHEQUES MADE PAYABLE TO MUIR HEWITT)
TELEPHONE FOR MORE DETAILS.
OPENING HOURS: TUESDAY - SATURDAY 10.00AM - 5.00PM
MUIR HEWITT, HALIFAX ANTIQUES CENTRE, QUEENS ROAD MILLS, QUEENS ROAD/GIBBET STREET,
HALIFAX, WEST YORKSHIRE, HX1 4LR
TEL/FAX: (01422) 347377 EVENINGS: (01274) 882051

ART • DECO • CERAMICS

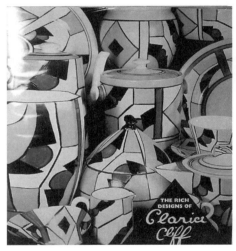